T0114077

Cambridge Elements ☰

Elements in Publishing and Book Culture
edited by
Samantha Rayner
University College London

PUBLISHING AGAINST APARTHEID SOUTH AFRICA

A Case Study of Ravan Press

Elizabeth le Roux
University of Pretoria

CAMBRIDGE
UNIVERSITY PRESS

University Printing House, Cambridge CB2 8BS, United Kingdom

One Liberty Plaza, 20th Floor, New York, NY 10006, USA

477 Williamstown Road, Port Melbourne, VIC 3207, Australia

314–321, 3rd Floor, Plot 3, Splendor Forum, Jasola District Centre,
New Delhi – 110025, India

79 Anson Road, #06–04/06, Singapore 079906

Cambridge University Press is part of the University of Cambridge.

It furthers the University's mission by disseminating knowledge in the pursuit of
education, learning, and research at the highest international levels of excellence.

www.cambridge.org
Information on this title: www.cambridge.org/9781108737753
DOI: 10.1017/9781108642736

First published 2020

A catalogue record for this publication is available from the British Library.

ISBN 978-1-108-73775-3 Paperback
ISSN 2514–8524 (online)
ISSN 2514–8516 (print)

Publishing against Apartheid South Africa

A Case Study of Ravan Press

Elements in Publishing and Book Culture

DOI: 10.1017/9781108642736

First published online: December 2020

Elizabeth le Roux

University of Pretoria

Author for correspondence: Elizabeth le Roux, beth.leroux@up.ac.za

ABSTRACT: In many parts of the world, oppositional publishing has emerged in contexts of state oppression. In South Africa, censorship laws were enacted in the 1960s, and the next decade saw increased pressure on freedom of speech and publishing. With growing restrictions on information, activist publishing emerged. These highly politicised publishers had a social responsibility to contribute to social change. In spite of their cultural, political and social importance, no academic study of their history has yet been undertaken. This Element aims to fill that gap by examining the history of the most vocal and arguably the most radical of this group, Ravan Press. Using archival material, interviews and the books themselves, the Element examines what the history of Ravan reveals about the role of oppositional print culture.

KEYWORDS: anti-apartheid, oppositional publishing, print culture, publishing history, Ravan Press

ISBNs: 9781108737753 (PB), 9781108642736 (OC)

ISSNs: 2514-8524 (online), 2514-8516 (print)

Contents

1 Publishing and Protest

In 1972, the political correspondent for the conservative newspaper *Hoofstad* described a visit to a Cape Town bookshop where liberal books were selling 'like hot cakes' and being 'devoured by young Bantus and white intellectuals'. While he deplored the books' contents, which included 'many statements which would make the Afrikaner's hair rise', he contrasted their covers, designs and low prices with the 'handful of books from Afrikaner intellectuals who support separate development', and which are 'not generally available, are expensive and have uninteresting hard covers'.[1] The reactions to anti-apartheid publishing differed widely, from *Hoofstad*'s qualified disapproval to overt denunciation ('a demonical movement originating from American Marxism') as well as firm support ('all that is left of sanity in a land gone mad').[2]

What is the role of a publisher in times of struggle or state oppression? Oppositional publishers seek the freedom to publish works that encourage debate and to change society itself. In South Africa, the apartheid state introduced strict limits on free speech and communications. With growing restrictions on what South African publishers could produce, and especially increasingly rigorous censorship laws, several highly politicised publishers were formed who saw a responsibility to transmit oppositional values through print. In spite of the cultural, political and social importance of such publishers, no academic study of their history has yet been undertaken. This book aims to fill that gap by examining the history of the most vocal and arguably the most radical of this group, Ravan Press.

At Ravan, publishing was a tool to fight against apartheid; in fact, publishing was a form of resistance in its own right. This was not a company founded to make a profit, but rather an activist organisation aiming to create awareness and shift people's beliefs. Like the black-owned presses in the Harlem Renaissance, Ravan was 'not interested in making money, but in publishing what needed to be published'.[3] Its mission was clear:

---

[1] *Hoofstad*, 28 April 1972.   [2] In Randall, *Taste of Power*.
[3] Young, *Black Writers*, 66.

> [W]e are part of that section of South African society
> engaged in changing the present social system. We see
> ourselves then as part of a process of change: we aim to
> produce books that inform the struggle in the present
> (through recovering our history or entering into the debates
> of the day) and that create a climate in which the new society
> can be discussed.[4]

Thus far, research on anti-apartheid resistance has highlighted political and to
some extent cultural engagement, with little attention being paid to print
culture. This book will trace the history of Ravan Press in the period between
1972 and 2000. Using archival material, interviews and the books themselves,
I focus on what the history of Ravan reveals about the role of a publisher in
social change: a balancing act between commercial viability and radical
publishing and between white ownership and black expression. The majority
of studies privilege the role of literature, but Ravan published both fiction and
non-fiction and had an important impact with both. Attention will thus be
paid to the publications list, mission and editorial philosophy, as well as the
politics informing the author and staff profiles, and Ravan's readership and
impact. Ravan was ultimately unable to survive South Africa's transition
period, amid changing political, social and economic conditions, in part
because of a lack of support from the new government. This has inhibited
the emergence of a free, diverse publishing industry in the post-apartheid era.

Theories of Engagement

While the role of the media in both amplifying and contesting power
dynamics has been studied, less scholarly attention has been paid to the
role of publishers. But publishers, whether producing books or periodicals,
fiction or non-fiction, are significant cultural and political mediators in their
own right. The media is accepted as having a role as a watchdog, a witness
to social protest; there are close relationships between modes of production;
media forms; and oppositional, participatory practice.[5] The media has also

---

[4] 'Opposition publishing in South Africa', undated report, Amazwi.

[5] Downing, *Alternative Communication*; Downing, *Radical Media*.

been shown to play a role in conflict and protest. If the mainstream media is a tool for either promoting or hampering democracy and development – what of the publishing of other forms of media, including books? The case examined here aims to extend our understanding of the political role of the media to include publishers. This also extends the view of publishing as operating in what Pierre Bourdieu[6] calls 'spheres of restricted or mass production', which are defined in terms of whether they privilege literary (or symbolic) capital or economic capital to a sphere which favoured political activism over either of these aspects.

Examining publishing houses and their operations also provides another lens for considering how power and ideology function in a society. Publishing – as its name suggests – takes place in a public sphere and reflects the inequalities existing in society. Often run by elites and aimed at small literate and educated groups, publishing is not inherently democratic – even mass-market publishing tends to promote elite values. Gatekeeping may focus on quality, but it also restricts the access of both authors and readers. However, once books are in the public sphere, they can become more subversive of existing power structures: they can be read by anyone who is literate; they can be smuggled and circulated under clandestine circumstances. The concept of 'opposition' can be related to Stuart Hall's categorisation of the different subject positions available to an audience receiving a message: dominant-hegemonic, negotiated and contrary.[7] Schweitzer echoes Hall, noting that in Spain during the Franco period, 'publishing houses had three major possibilities for their orientation: a direction remaining ideologically close to the regime, neutrality or opposition.'[8] The two poles have also been called a choice between 'confrontation and capitulation'.[9] When a publisher actively works to subvert the norms of a society, then there is a possibility for dissenting voices to be heard, for networks to be created and for books to tell a story that the mainstream regime would prefer to keep untold. This in turn can lead to a greater awareness of social injustice and thus social change. Describing oppositional publishers in Portugal, Nuno Medeiros remarks that

[6] Bourdieu, 'Market of Symbolic Goods'.   [7] Hall, 'Encoding/Decoding', 517.

[8] Schweitzer, 'Spanish publishing houses'.

[9] Hacksley, 'An Oppositional Publisher'.

their operations reflect 'a publisher's social role in the construction of print culture and in the forms in which that print culture can interfere in the context and be influenced by it'.[10] Rachael Schreiber calls this 'print activism'.[11]

I call these publishers 'oppositional' but the terms used vary widely: alternative, subversive, anti-establishment, left wing, radical, interventionist or progressive – even, broadly, independent publishing. Alternative publishing, according to Cloete, is 'a fairly loose concept. Broadly defined, it includes anything outside mainstream commercial publishing, where the market is the final determinant of what is published. In contrast, [in alternative publishing] the publishing mission takes precedence over the business mission.'[12] The publisher David Philip used the term 'oppositional' to describe publishing that is 'anti-apartheid and pro-conservation'.[13] Similarly, in countries as diverse as Turkey and Portugal, oppositional publishing has been associated with dissident views: 'books with radical substance and content'.[14]

Enzensberger has proposed a politically emancipatory use of media characterised by interaction between audiences and creators, collective production and a concern with everyday life.[15] These categories map closely onto the criteria developed by the Alternatives in Print project, for classifying alternative publishers: these are non-commercial, demonstrating that 'a basic concern for ideas, not the concern for profit, is the motivation for publication'; their publications should focus on 'social responsibility or creative expression, or usually a combination of both'.[16] For instance, at British publishers such as New Beacon Books and Bogle L'Ouverture, the political mission of publishing by, for and about black people was prioritised over the commercial mission.[17] Oppositional publishers, then, can play an agenda-setting role, similar to that of the media. While small in size and output – and often barely meeting their costs – they

---

[10]   Medeiros, 'Action, Reaction and Protest', 148.
[11]   Schreiber, ed. *Modern Print Activism*.   [12]   Cloete, 'Alternative Publishing', 43.
[13]   Philip, 'Book Publishing'.
[14]   Albert, 'Alternative publishing'; Maués, 'Livros, editoras e oposiçã'.
[15]   Enzensberger, 'Theory of the Media'.   [16]   ALA, *Alternatives in Print*, vii.
[17]   Ireland, 'Laying the Foundations'.

may have a disproportionate visibility and impact in shaping attitudes and behaviour. The general problems of independent publishers, such as financial difficulties and hostility from mainstream distribution channels, are also those of oppositional publishers, although the latter face additional obstacles in the form of political repression. In contrast with the underground media, however, they do not necessarily employ underground distribution networks, although they may experiment with dissemination techniques that take them beyond mainstream bookselling circuits.[18]

Such publishers often follow a collectivist process of production and experiment with form and content. Their lack of hierarchy enables them to work closely with authors and readers, highlighting the value of collective production – their staff may see themselves, like alternative journalists, as activists rather than professionals. Describing the underground press in the United States, McMillian argues, 'Lacking any pretense of objectivity, [writers] put across forcefully opinionated accounts of events that mattered deeply to them.'[19] A similar lack of neutrality has been identified among radical French publishers, who present themselves as partisan, 'without moderation'; they aim to *'faire entendre des voix différentes, face aux forces de la domination qui exercent une police de la pensée'* ('to make different voices heard, in the face of dominating forces that seek to police thinking').[20] French studies of engaged publishing outline their role as participating in public debate, providing citizens with the information they need about their society.[21] Alternative publishers may maintain close links with radical organisations, which adds to their perceived legitimacy among their audience.

Context

Oppositional publishing has thus been encountered in various places in times of repression. In South Africa, it arose in resistance to the apartheid regime. The Nationalist government had an impact on all spheres of life and sought brutally to minimise dissent. After the Sharpeville massacres of 1960, a host of

---

[18] Schweitzer, 'Spanish publishing houses'.

[19] McMillian, *Smoking Typewriters*, 4.

[20] Douyère & Pinhas, 'L'accès à la parole', 76.

[21] Douyère & Pinhas, 'L'accès à la parole', 76.

political organisations were banned. With cultural production being seen as deeply embedded in and inextricably linked with politics, cultural organisations were driven underground, authors proscribed or jailed and journals closed down. The government's attitude to dissenting views led it to develop a raft of legislation and restrictions to control the publication and distribution of publications. The framework was a system of post-publication censorship, regulated by the Publications and Entertainments Act (1963), amended in 1974, leading to a huge rise in the number of books banned for being 'undesirable': '[i]n 1948, 100 titles were banned by the new apartheid government; by 1971 this number had grown dramatically to about 18 000.'[22] The system was effective, even if not entirely consistent, leading to what has been called a 'decade of black silence' in the 1960s.[23]

But resistance was also on the rise. In the 1970s, the government faced a renewed wave of resistance, with labour unrest, economic boycotts and protests that culminated in the Soweto uprising of 1976. There was also an increase in philosophical and cultural resistance, exemplified in the rise of Black Consciousness. As expressed by exponents such as Steve Biko and Bennie Khoapa, Black Consciousness was a movement actively attempting to reclaim black identity. Integral to this attempt was the use of cultural and intellectual channels: 'culture was the means through which the psychological battle would be fought,' Biko explained in a 1971 paper on 'Some African Cultural Concepts'.[24] It was strongly believed that 'Forms such as literature could be used to expose social conditions and the true nature of apartheid, allow individuals to express their emotional anger at denigration, and promote the spread of the message of Black Consciousness among a black audience.'[25] The writer Mbulelo Mzamane argues, 'Before the rise of the writers and artists of the Black Consciousness era, most of whom had been in their early teens during the Sharpeville crisis, there was as much stagnation on the cultural scene in South Africa as there was on the political front.'[26] Now, however, cultural groups started forming in place of political groups, as a base for mobilisation and collective action.

---

[22] Suttie, 'Formative years', 112. [23] Kantey, 'Publishing in South Africa', xii.

[24] Penfold, 'Black Consciousness', 57. [25] Sole, 'Political Fiction', 101.

[26] Mzamane, 'Impact of Black Consciousness', 180.

The purpose of such cultural activity was resistance and social change. Artists and writers were 'cultural workers', using their texts to disseminate political ideas: 'Art cannot overthrow government, but it can inspire change,' as the saying went.[27] Ravan's journal, *Staffrider*, called this 'art [that] seeks *intentionally* to engage itself in a challenging and critical way with the social and political realities of its time and place. It does more than simply *reflect* the society which gives rise to it; it expresses a social or political message.'[28] The writer Mafika Gwala described writing as a 'cultural weapon'.[29] Mzamane was no less militant, arguing that

> since the most important lessons for South Africans are in the political sphere, a writer in that land is unimportant, irrelevant and probably alienated unless he is political. Art and politics in South Africa, as in many parts of Africa, have become inseparable for the simple reason that politics pervades all aspects of a Blackman's existence.[30]

This sense of mission led to writing focused on witness, documentary and protest or what Es'kia Mphahlele called a 'hard apocalyptic voice'.[31] This view contrasts with that of many white writers of the time, who believed that nothing should impinge on a writer's freedom of expression:

> Insist[ing] on artistic freedom, [white writers] elect to attack writers committed to political and socio-cultural change as well as freedom for all. . . . Blinded by the desire to retain the cultural high ground, their refusal to participate in the struggle for social change is directly related to a disenabling and narrow view of freedom.[32]

---

[27] Kellner & Gonzalez, eds, *Thami Mnyele + Medu*, 88.

[28] *Staffrider* 3(4) (1980), 14 (emphasis in original).

[29] Gwala, 'Writing as a Cultural Weapon'.

[30] Mzamane, *New Classic* 5 (1978), 42.

[31] In Chapman, 'The year that was (1981)', 169.

[32] Oliphant, 'Forums and Forces', 97.

This was an important debate among writers, which was not resolved so much as it died away after the end of apartheid.

But these writers could not effect social change on their own: they needed a platform. They needed, in short, a publisher. Sipho Sepamla, writing in the *New Classic* in 1976, pointed to an absence of publishing opportunities: 'A problem that wears us down . . . is lack of publishers and outlets. . . . There is not a single black publisher I know of in this country.'[33] In the early 1970s, a number of new publishers formed, including David Philip, Ravan, Bateleur and Taurus. By the early 1980s, Michael Chapman could celebrate seeing 'more established writers, many of whom were published abroad before the existence of viable local publishing opportunities, also turning their support to the South African industry'.[34]

Oppositional publishers cannot escape their context. Working in a stratified society, they are criticised if their own organisation remains too segregated, or if one group is perceived to be favoured over another. Issues of ownership and control are almost always contentious, even in an apparently democratic organisation. John K. Young notes in the US context that 'what sets the white publisher–black author relationship apart is the underlying social structure that transforms the usual unequal relationship into an extension of a much deeper cultural dynamic.'[35] His work illustrates the extent to which black authors have negotiated white power structures. Much of what Young describes applies equally to the South African situation: the vast majority of publishers were – and remain – white owned and managed. A related problem is language: the medium of publication was English. This was seen as necessary to reach the international community but was a compromise in a context where Afrikaans and English were both languages of colonisation and oppression. However, the oppositional publishers aimed not to perpetuate divides among racial groups but to overcome them – indeed, to overthrow a racially oppressive government in so doing. In an attempt to free themselves from what they saw as white patronage, some black authors established their own publishers, such as BLAC (Black Literature and Arts Congress) and Skotaville.

---

[33] Sepamla, 'The Black Writer', 119.   [34] Chapman, 'The year that was (1982)'.
[35] Young, *Black Writers*, 4.

Moreover, the common problems of financial hardship and acting on the periphery of a mainstream publishing industry persisted: 'The challenges were great. The writers were unknown, the price of the books had to be kept low for popular appeal; most of all the books were often banned resulting in enormous financial losses.'[36] More commercial publishing houses, seeing the initial success of the new black writers, sought to co-opt such authors for profit. In hindsight, it is remarkable that the oppositional publishers survived at all, and the fact that they declined after the political transition from apartheid seems inevitable.

Patrick McGuiness writes, 'We assume that politics is action. But politics is also, and perhaps more so, language: manifesto, declaration, exhortation, persuasion, assertion.'[37] Publishing plays an important role in social change. By showing how one publisher operated, strategised and built communities, this book contributes to our understanding of the role of oppositional print culture as part of the anti-apartheid struggle. The chapters follow a broadly chronological path.

2 Beginnings

Spro-cas

The author J.M. Coetzee had received a number of rejections of his debut novel when he submitted the manuscript to Ravan Press in 1973. He knew nothing about Ravan 'except that it had been in trouble with the government, which was a good sign, and that it had some kind of Christian background, which was not necessarily a good sign'.[38] At about the same time, when Miriam Tlali sought a publisher for her first novel, she wrote to John Rees at the South African Council of Churches and he recommended Ravan Press. Who was this publisher, both Christian and activist, who would publish both the first work of an author who went on to become a Nobel laureate and a novel by the first black woman published in South Africa?

---

[36] Barnett, *A Vision of Order*, 39.   [37] McGuinness, *Poetry and Radical Politics*.
[38] McDonald, *The Literature Police*, 106.

Ravan Press emerged from a Christian project: Beyers Naude, the dissident cleric, set up the Christian Institute and then established the Study Project on Christianity in Apartheid Society (Spro-cas) in 1969 to investigate 'practicable and morally acceptable alternatives to apartheid'.[39] He appointed Peter Randall, a former teacher and assistant director of the South African Institute for Race Relations, as director. Print culture was central to the work of Spro-cas, which billed itself as 'a South African publishing venture of considerable importance'.[40] Recognising that the apartheid state used restrictions on information, censorship and propaganda to maintain its hold on power, the project produced reports that critiqued discrimination, inequality and domination. These were not neutral by any means; they have been described as a combination of propaganda and analysis.[41] However, while the authors were all opposed to apartheid, they represented a diversity of views, from the liberal politics of Alan Paton and the United Party to the more radical protests of Rick Turner and the Black Consciousness Movement (BCM).

Randall has been described as having the 'perfect curriculum vitae for the director of Spro-Cas . . . although he was not particularly religious': he had a liberal background, a wide network and experience in research and publication.[42] Correspondence in the archives shows him active in every aspect of the work. Beside him, Reverend Danie van Zyl managed production and helped with promotion. Not wanting to run the risk of using commercial printers who did not support their political views, printing was done in-house: 'Beyers had motivated for a printing press from the Dutch and German church sponsors of our work. This proved an exceptionally fortuitous investment as many commercial printers refused to print our material because they were intimidated by visits from [the Security Police] who threatened them if they printed for us.'[43] In-house printing also helped save costs and keep prices low. The reports were also designed in-house,

---

[39]   Randall, ed. *Anatomy of Apartheid*, 5.

[40]   Randall to newspaper editors, 28 January 1971, 1998.8.33.1, Amazwi.

[41]   Stadler, 'Anxious radicals', 102.   [42]   Stadler, 'Anxious radicals', 102.

[43]   Kleinschmidt, 'Roots and journeys', 9.

with Van Zyl using one of the first automated phototypesetters in South Africa.[44]

The reports were widely advertised and reviewed and sold almost three times more than expected – 'a quite astonishing demand'.[45] The readership was diverse; students, academics and clerics formed the majority.[46] Public responses varied. Supporters argued that 'All South Africans who are committed to bringing about change in our society should read the Spro-cas reports,' and that 'its impact on political thought in South Africa has been considerable.'[47] Some newspaper editors were sympathetic but admitted that they were under pressure not to mention Spro-cas. Government supporters denounced a perceived hidden agenda: 'Much more cleverly disguised and therefore much more sinister . . . the Spro-cas missionaries have been the chief purveyors of the myths of Black Theology and Black Consciousness.'[48] Seeking to stifle this dissenting agenda, the government imposed a variety of controls, with both direct and indirect effects: barriers to distribution, leading to refusals to review publications in mainstream media and to stock them in bookshops; the banning of authors and books; and financial losses due to bannings.[49] A banning created restrictions on people's movements and activities; for instance, they had little freedom of association and could not be published or even quoted in a published book. Moreover, it was a punishable offence to own or distribute a book that contained the writings of a banned person. This meant that in the report *Some Implications of Inequality*, a chapter by the Reverend Cosmos Desmond had to be cut after his banning. To highlight this self-censorship, the book appeared with a number of blank pages.

Some critics charge that the reports were paternalistic and reached a limited, mainly white, community. It is true that the programme was dominated by white liberal academics. This may in part be due to the split in Spro-cas II, into

---

[44] Danie van Zyl, interview with author, 30 January 2019.
[45] Randall to Rev. Godfrey Wilson, 27 May 1971, 1998.8.33.2, Amazwi.
[46] Randall to William Drennan, 1 February 1971, 1998.8.33.2, Amazwi.
[47] *Black Sash Journal*, August 1972; Marie Dyer, *Reality*, January 1974, 1998.8.33.2, Amazwi.
[48] Editorial, *The Education Journal*, September 1973.
[49] Randall, 'Some publishing problems', 75–78.

a Black Community Programme (run by Bennie Khoapa and Steve Biko) and a White Consciousness Programme. Randall candidly admitted that 'The white staff of Spro-cas see our task as primarily within the white community, to prepare it for fundamental change, and to bring about such meaningful reform as possible.'[50] Horst Kleinschmidt, who joined Spro-cas II, is more critical: 'Our aim was to get whites who morally rejected apartheid to take a stand and do something ... we were talking to a very small converted crowd.'[51] He also later noted that 'the CI[52] was very white', and ideologically divided: 'Steve Biko would argue strongly in favour of a socialist state, and Peter Randall would find it much easier to argue in favour of a liberal structure.' At the same time, he sums up Spro-cas as 'radical' rather than 'liberal': 'it was in my view an organisation which was closer to opposing and resisting apartheid than anything I knew in South Africa at the time.'[53]

The publications produced by the Black Community Programme were different – they featured entirely black authors and aimed at creating awareness among a black readership. These included *Black Viewpoint* and *Black Review*, a comprehensive survey of black organisations and activities. In the latter, Khoapa noted the need for black publishing houses: 'Concern has been expressed by most groups that blacks will never communicate effectively until they control their own medium.'[54] As such, *Black Review* was emblematic of the struggle for a black voice against white paternalism.[55]

Broader Publishing

Given the lack of black-controlled publishers, it became increasingly clear that there was a need for a new kind of publishing house. In the absence of other radical publishers, 'many writers were viewing Spro-cas as a publisher in its own right and were submitting manuscripts for

---

[50] Randall, 'Motivations and assumptions', 5.

[51] Kleinschmidt, interview with Julie Frederikse, 1986, South African History Online.

[52] CI is the Christian Institute, the larger body under which Spro-cas fell.

[53] Kleinschmidt, interview with Julie Frederikse, 1986, South African History Online.

[54] Khoapa, *Black Review*, 44.   [55] Hadfield, *Liberation and Development*, 64.

consideration.'[56] 'We realised,' Randall says, 'there was a need for some kind of agency to do this kind of publishing, loosely defined as material relating to South African issues, race, economics, politics and social change. Then gradually we found poets and prose writers turning to us and we began to publish work quite distinct from the socio/political things we were doing.'[57] He and Van Zyl thus proposed a company 'to publish in the interests of social justice' – 'a publishing firm that will do the stuff that nobody else will'.[58] Spro-cas began to publish works that traditional publishers would not consider.

Before the Spro-cas reports were even finalised, Rick Turner's anarchistic vision of a future society, *The Eye of the Needle: An essay on participatory democracy*, was produced in May 1972. Like many oppositional publications, it was by a white male academic, but Turner was more closely aligned with radical politics and Black Consciousness than most. *Eye of the Needle* was utopian, but Randall defended it as 'a serious attempt to relate the values of Christianity to the structures of our society'.[59] It was also influential, serving 'to shift the focus of opposition debate',[60] and had a long-lasting impact as a 'political primer [providing] a deeper and philosophical content for many in our generation . . . mostly to young white and black trade union activists and to those whose radicalism needed a philosophical foundation'.[61]

The second title was a set of 'protest poems' by James Matthews and Gladys Thomas. *Cry Rage!* was an experimental publication, with no pagination. Alvarez-Pereyre describes it as an 'explosion of a vengeful anger and the promise of retribution' and 'the expression of a South African version of Black Power'.[62] As a result, according to Matthews, it was 'the first book of poetry discussed in parliament by the *Herrenvolk* lawmakers. They could not decide whether it was poetry or a political bomb.'[63] Both *Eye of the Needle* and *Cry Rage!* sold briskly before being banned in

---

[56] Randall, 'Beginnings of Ravan Press'. [57] Nicol, 'Ravan flies out of the red'.

[58] Van Zyl, interview. [59] Randall, quoted in Rich, *Hope and Despair*, 108.

[60] Morphet, 'Introduction'. [61] Kleinschmidt, 'Roots and journeys', 10–11.

[62] Alvarez-Pereyre, *The Poetry of Commitment*, 214.

[63] Matthews to Randall, 3 March 1975. PMA

March 1973. At first, Randall decided not to appeal the bannings, both on principle and because of the expense.[64] The greater outcry about Turner's banning created a perception that the books were valued differently: when *Cry Rage!* was banned, 'there were no petitions signed by the white intelligentsia, there were no vociferous shoutings by the white liberal press, and no fund was established to help the proscribed writers by taking the matter to court.'[65] Matthews' next book, published by his own start-up, BLAC, suffered the same fate.

Randall and Van Zyl soon became familiar with the processes of banning. In fact, they worked knowing that books would be banned:

> So we would work to get a manuscript to book in 24 hours, working through the night. The work would be typeset but then pasted up manually, printed on the Heidelberg, bound by hand, and then posted out to a list of 60–80 people who got copies (and were asked to pay if they could, but did not have to), as well as all the newspapers. So, if the book was banned on Friday, when the Government Gazette came out, we aimed to have at least 100 copies that had gone out.[66]

Kleinschmidt adds, 'We took delight in surreptitiously continuing with distributing banned copies for the [security police] had failed to confiscate all copies at our premises.'[67] The bannings meant financial losses, but they also created publicity and visibility for the publishing programme.

Why did a Christian publishing programme include radical non-fiction and poetry in its list? Their inclusion, and evident popularity, leads us to consider how a more ambitious publishing entity emerged from Spro-cas. Two significant factors may later be traced in Ravan's publishing list: the 'open-ended, exploratory mode and its willingness to move from the realm of religion to the secular worlds of sociology, politics, education, and

---

[64] Randall to Raymond Tucker, 16 March 1973. PMA

[65] Oswald Mtshali, in Chapman, 'The year that was (1982)', 109.

[66] Van Zyl, interview. [67] Kleinschmidt, 'Roots and journeys', 14.

economics' and 'bringing religious and secular voices from different traditions into conversation'.[68]

Launching Ravan

Late in 1972, Ravan Press (Pty) Ltd was launched, with Naudé, Van Zyl and Randall as directors. The name was formed from the initial letters of their names, not the bird selected for the logo.[69] Van Zyl was the first director, while Randall was busy wrapping up Spro-cas. 'Beyers was never really involved,' says Van Zyl, 'He was the PR man. He brought in lots of contacts from overseas. He also brought in some specific jobs (some more printing than publishing).'[70] His name is almost absent from the archives as a result.

Ravan was set up as a printer but also a future channel for publishing. A Spro-cas report notes, 'Ravan Press was established to meet the production needs of such material [for social change] and it is intended that the press should continue as an independent publishing and communications company after Spro-cas itself ends.'[71] As a result, the press has been variously described as 'an outgrowth of the Christian Institute's printing unit'[72] and 'the printing and publishing arm of the Christian Institute',[73] although Randall pointedly makes the distinction that it was *not* a 'child of the Christian Institute [but] an organic outgrowth of the Spro-cas publishing programme'.[74] It was both a printer and a publisher: its primary objective was to 'print the Spro-cas commissions' reports'[75] but also 'to publish Spro-cas' radical research.'[76] This has created confusion about who exactly was publishing what and when. Bibliographies list the books as being published by Spro-cas or Ravan Press, interchangeably, or sometimes just printed by Ravan. This confusion worked

---

[68] Dubow, *Apartheid 1948–1994*, 168–9.

[69] According to sources, a Penguin designer produced the logo as a contribution to the struggle in South Africa.

[70] Van Zyl interview. [71] Spro-cas, 'Future plans', 1972, 1988.8.33, Amazwi.

[72] Randall, *Taste of Power*, 131. [73] ALAP, *Interim Report*, 18.

[74] De Waal, 'Ravan will NOT close'. [75] Cloete, 'Alternative publishing', 47.

[76] Mpe & Seeber, 'Politics of Book Publishing', 25; see also Moss, 'Life and changing times', 144–6.

to Ravan's advantage in 1974, when the directors were prosecuted under the Suppression of Communism Act for publishing the words of a banned person, Paul Pretorius of the National Union of South African Students (NUSAS). The case was dismissed on a technicality because the Security Police could not distinguish between Spro-cas (as publisher) and Ravan Press (as printer).

Ravan's list thus cannot immediately be distinguished from that of Spro-cas. Costing was worked out on an ad hoc basis, with no imperative to make a profit. There was little active decision-making – books came in through an existing network of friends and colleagues. For instance, Ravan began working with the literary magazine *Ophir* based on a friendship with Peter Horn and Walter Saunders. The *Ophir* connection also led to a close relationship with the small literary publisher Bateleur, run by Lionel Abrahams and Patrick Cullinan. After some co-publishing ventures, Abrahams 'decided to throw my lot in with Ravan Press on terms that include their purchase of our book stock'.[77] The arrangement brought several new authors to Ravan.

When Wopko Jensma, who had published in *Ophir*, wanted to produce a book of poems and woodcuts, he approached his close friend Van Zyl.[78] *Sing for our Execution* was published by Ophir/Ravan in May 1973, typeset by the author himself.[79] The book had an immediate impact: Lionel Abrahams observed, 'At a time when people are more than ever aware of their colour, even in the arts, Wopko Jensma is the only South African artist in any medium who has transcended the barriers. His work is neither English nor Afrikaans, black nor white.'[80] In 1975, Jensma's next volume of poetry, *Where White is the Colour, Where Black is the Number* was also published by Ravan. This work was banned. The censor's report by M.G. Scholtz was highly critical, finding it inexplicable that a publisher could accept such a work when their function was to separate the wheat from the chaff: '*die kaf van die korrels te skei.*'[81] In an interview following the banning, Jensma said: 'To have one's book banned in this country is to be given a literary prize, it is at least some indication that people are reading one's

77 Abrahams to Ad Donker, 31 August 1977, 2008.13.5.131, Amazwi.
78 Van Zyl, interview. 79 Sheik, 'Biographical study of Wopko Jensma'.
80 Lionel Abrahams, *Rand Daily Mail*, 6 January 1975.
81 Kleyn & Marais, 'Wopko Jensma en die sensuurwetgewing'.

work and one should take it as an honour.'[82] Ravan also published his third collection, *I Must Show You My Clippings* (1977).

After Jensma's work came what Randall calls 'the black books' – Nadine Gordimer's *The Black Interpreters*, Chabani Manganyi's *Being-Black-in-the-World* and Peter Walshe's *Black Nationalism in South Africa*. The title pages still reflect the Spro-cas link, although the authors' contracts were with Ravan Press. It may seem quite a coup for such a young publisher to publish a writer of Gordimer's reputation, but she was on the Ravan board and published with them, in Randall's words, 'out of charity'.[83] Manganyi's and Walshe's works had a 'huge influence on a young generation of left-leaning, anti-apartheid, mostly white, aspiring academics and intellectuals'.[84]

The year 1974 saw the first full year of publishing under the Ravan imprint: one novel, four poetry collections, a play and three non-fiction titles. With the Spro-cas funding coming to an end, the printer was sold to become a profit-making concern.[85] Van Zyl took up a new posting as a priest, and Randall stepped into the role of director. He was supported by a staff of fourteen, including the writer Rose Zwi, who worked as an editor, Pat Schwartz as proofreader and Glenda Webster as accountant. Designers included Jackie Bosman and Merle Stoltenkamp, both of whom had to learn how to typeset. The staff were often 'chaotically busy'.[86] Randall took most of the editorial decisions himself and did much of the editing. He has been described as the 'liberal guardian' of the list', and Peter McDonald suggests that he had a 'prudently pragmatic approach' to publishing and was part of the 'dominant white liberal culture'.[87] He has also been critically referred to in correspondence as '*Baas* Randall'.[88] It is true that his attitude was somewhat paternalistic.

---

[82] In Sheik, 'Biographical study of Wopko Jensma'.

[83] Peter Randall, interview with author, May 2017.

[84] Hayes, 'Chabani Manganyi', 74.

[85] Ravan continued to work with Zenith Printers, as it became known. 'The bind in publishing', *Financial Mail*, 19 July 1974, 226.

[86] Berchowitz to T.G. Rosenthal, 17 February 1978, 1998.8.1, Amazwi.

[87] McDonald, *Literature Police*, 136.

[88] [Authors' letter], 19 April 1977, 2014.256.8.1.31, Amazwi. 'Baas' is an Afrikaans term for 'boss' or 'master'.

But he was also responsible for highly experimental and pioneering publishing, especially in promoting the voices of black writers, and he promoted authors whose views were far more radical than his own.[89]

Randall's view of the role of writers and publishers in the struggle is similar to that espoused by Gordimer, as he noted, 'The kind of titles a publisher puts out will reflect his interests and I am interested in social change in South Africa.'[90] He went on:

> [T]rue literature and art will continue to transcend any ideology, with personal integrity as their criterion. As interpreters who crystallise the issues and communicate their significance, artists have the very important function of relating to all those who themselves have integrity in relating to others irrespective of colour. Artists are able to interpret our situation and speak to people of all groups in a universal medium and in a way that academics, journalists and clergy cannot because they are so firmly labelled in their ethnic or denominational boxes.[91]

A draft publicity leaflet shows the staff wrestling with the mission: "the book is published by Ravan Press Johannesburg, which specialises in ~~indigenous~~ contemporary South African writing, both fiction and non-fiction, and carries forward the work of Spro-cas. . . . Ravan Press publishes relevant books on contemporary social issues.'[92] The focus thus fell on relevance, commitment and urgency – 'Books about South Africa and its people NOW' – a difficult list to market. After 1976, Gillian Berchowitz was hired as sales manager and found that 'the large majority of South Africans weren't interested in serious books about South African politics and it was hard going.'[93] She saw the primary audience as liberal, middle-class whites, partly because of the difficulties of accessing books among black South

---

[89] Keaney, 'From the Sophiatown Shebeens', 227.

[90] Nicol, 'Ravan flies out of the red'. [91] Randall, *Taste of Power*, 81.

[92] Production material, 1998.8.10.2, Amazwi.

[93] Gillian Berchowitz, email to author, 29 March 2017.

Africans. Moreover, bookshops would stock nothing controversial. Randall lamented: 'I sometimes think only lunatics try to publish anything other than travel guides and gardening books in this country!'[94]

Through a combination of good judgement and luck, Ravan had several notable 'firsts'. For instance, in October 1973, Randall recalls taking a manuscript home and reading it through in a single sitting: 'My sober judgement was that this unsolicited manuscript by an unknown author, which had been rejected everywhere else, was the work of a writer of genius.'[95] He immediately responded that he was 'in no doubt as to its quality and significance' and was eager to publish *Dusklands*.[96] Randall admits that he was an 'amateur publisher' who let the author get his way in most decisions. But J.M. Coetzee was also a very difficult author, refusing to provide biographical details and submitting an inappropriate author photo but also involving himself in every aspect of production, from blurbs to cover designs. When *Dusklands* appeared in 1974, Randall wrote to booksellers: 'I believe this book is so important, that I am bringing it to your notice now. I am proud to be associated with its publication.'[97] Ravan gambled on a large print run of 4 500 copies; however, unlike other titles printed in equally large numbers, the work was both a commercial and critical success – Ravan's best-selling work in 1975. As histories of Coetzee's publishing have shown, the success of this debut meant that he was able to interest an international publisher, Secker & Warburg, in his work.[98] Out of loyalty, he negotiated English-language rights for the South African market for Ravan for several titles. Randall plaintively notes, 'It was painful to know that as a small publisher we could not compete with international houses to retain authors for whom we had taken the initial risks.'[99]

Ravan was also a pioneer in publishing black writers. In particular, it was among the first to publish a black South African woman writer, Miriam Tlali, who had struggled to find a receptive publisher. Randall admits that he did not publish her novel because of its merit – he describes the original

[94] Randall to T.G. Rosenthal, 20 July 1977, 1998.8.1, Amazwi.
[95] Quoted in De Waal, 'Ravan will NOT close'.
[96] Randall to Coetzee, 2 November 1973, 1998.8.1, Amazwi.
[97] Randall to newspaper editors, March 1974, 1998.8.1, Amazwi.
[98] Kannemeyer, *J.M. Coetzee*, 235.   [99] Randall, 'The beginning of Ravan Press', 9.

manuscript for *Muriel at Metropolitan* as unpublishable – but for its novelty value. Although at the time she had little power to contest decisions to cut or reshape the novel, Tlali later condemned Ravan for reducing her work 'to shreds'.[100] Poets such as Motshile Nthodi seem to have had a happier experience, although his book, *To The Calabash*, took four years to be published. The Mofolo-Plomer Prize, established by Nadine Gordimer to promote unpublished local authors, further boosted the work of black authors. The first prize was jointly awarded in 1976 to two Ravan titles: Mbulelo Mzamane's collection of short stories, *Mzala*, and Peter Wilhelm's novel, *An Island Full of Grass*. Randall has spoken of several other authors whom he felt proud to publish, although their work may be less well known today – such as David Muller's darkly humorous short stories, *Whitey*.

Alongside the burgeoning fiction list, Ravan continued to publish social and political analysis. The oppositional mission can be seen in titles such as *The Trial of Beyers Naude*, with a chapter on the Ravan Press/Spro-cas trial, and even more clearly in the publication of papers from the Black Renaissance Convention, just weeks after the Soweto Uprisings of June 1976. This manifesto called directly for political action against the apartheid regime. The cleric Allan Boesak's *Farewell to Innocence* in 1977 examined Black Consciousness, linking it in this case to black theology. In an attempt to circumvent the censors, some copies were mailed directly to members of the mailing list, who could then decide whether to order or return the book. This was not a successful tactic, as David Philip also found.

Randall described Ravan in 1975 as 'very small and somewhat precarious'.[101] The main challenge, from the beginning, was keeping the press afloat: as with other independent publishers, it was difficult to achieve commercial viability. Rumours persisted that Ravan was on the verge of collapse. Publishing Peter Horn's *Walking Through Our Sleep*, Randall noted: 'You will have heard various reports about Ravan Press: the position is that we are trying to carry on the publishing, as funds become available.'[102] Similarly, after Coetzee wrote asking whether Ravan

---

[100] Le Roux, 'Miriam Tlali and Ravan Press'.
[101] Randall to Anthony Toyne, 10 November 1975, 1998.8.8.1, Amazwi.
[102] Randall to Peter Horn, 27 May 1974. PMA

was closing, Randall responded: 'Please disregard the rumour. Ravan Press is less likely to fold now than at any time in the past two years.'[103] After this optimism, the economic impact of the Soweto Uprisings was clearly felt, when just a few months later another author was told that his book would be delayed: 'I am afraid we shall not be able to get the book out this year after all, as our financial position simply will not permit this. The whole book trade is depressed, & we have just had our worst month, in terms of sales, for nearly two years.'[104] Balancing the books and maintaining cash flow was difficult, even with low overheads. In the mid-1970s, it cost about R1 000 a month to run Ravan. In a good month, sales amounted to two to three times the costs. With no capital behind it, the press was completely reliant on sales to remain sustainable. Randall has described the 'intense idealism' that ensured that 'the profit motive did not feature at all'.[105] David Philip notes, 'Most oppositional publishers have been largely funded from abroad and usually classify themselves as non-profitmaking.'[106] While this confers some freedom in publishing decisions – allowing 'the financial risk of dabbling in odd ventures and as a result discover new authors'[107] – there was no safety net. Moreover, contrary to perceptions, Ravan attempted to make its way without external funding: 'The government was bleeding us dry but we refused foreign money. We were unbelievably idealistic at first.'[108]

In place of foreign funding, subsidies were sought, either from trusts such as the Anglo-American Corporation's Chairman's Fund or from authors themselves. A policy was introduced to recoup costs before paying the maximum royalty suggested by the South African Publishers' Association, at 15 per cent. A typical letter of request summarises the position:

> We ourselves would like to undertake publication, but are
> faced with the problem that books of this nature are seldom

[103] Coetzee to Randall, 26 March 1976; Randall to Coetzee, 29 March 1976, 1998.8.1, Amazwi.

[104] Randall to David Muller, 31 August 1976, 1998.8.49, Amazwi.

[105] Randall, 'The beginnings of Ravan Press', 2.

[106] Philip, 'Book publishing', 45. [107] Greyling, 'Redefining the dialogue', 56.

[108] Randall, interview.

financially viable propositions, a problem which is exacer-
bated by the present economic position of the book trade.
Ravan Press is thus seeking assistance in the form of
a subsidy which would reduce our financial risk in this
project and would also enable us to market this book at
a price which would be attractive enough to make the book
marketable.[109]

Some funding has been ascribed to Walter Felgate, a sociologist at the
University of Natal with political connections. There were rumours that he
had access to vast amounts of money, but no certainty as to its source. With
Ravan needing capital, he bought out the shares owned by Naude and Van
Zyl and then produced subventions for certain titles. Staff have asserted,
'Nobody had any idea who he was and what he was up to or where his
money came from. He claimed to have his own money from his time at Rio
Tinto Zinc (a large multinational mining company), but he alluded to other
money sources as well – MI5? CIA? Who knew?'[110] His involvement also
brought in George Shuttleworth, an engineer, who later claimed to be the
majority shareholder in Ravan and held his own, one-man director's meetings. In about 1978, Derek Beatty (of Zenith Printers) and Shuttleworth are
listed on letterheads as directors of Ravan Press. None of the other staff
seem sure of their role, and the archives provide no answers.

State Harassment

The fluctuating income from sales can be directly linked to censorship. In
particular, the risks and costs increased when books were banned. For
instance, when Fatima Meer was banned in terms of the Internal Security
Act in 1976, Ravan had to withdraw three publications from circulation. 'The
only way they can now be sold in South Africa,' Daniel Kunene lamented, 'is
by having these chapters physically torn or cut out.'[111] Randall told
a journalist: 'A couple more bannings and we're going to be in real trouble.
We've had four titles banned outright and 16 other books affected by the

---

[109] Randall to various funders, 1977, 1998.8.30, Amazwi.
[110] Berchowitz, email message. [111] Kunene, 'Ideas under Arrest', 221.

banning of individuals, books that had to be reprinted or chapters and passages blacked out.'[112] By 1975, Ravan's losses were around R20 000 as a result of bannings, on an annual budget of R35 000, with losses on Jensma's book alone amounting to nearly R5 000. A knock-on effect was uncertainty over the forward publishing schedule; in 1975, Randall wrote to Manganyi:

> The banning in quick succession of two of our books has hit
> us hard, and a pending Supreme Court trial looms later this
> month. So we have reluctantly decided to suspend publish-
> ing of all new books other than those already in press. I can
> only hope that this position will improve next year.[113]

Did this uncertainty lead to less risk-taking? Randall argued: 'Under no circumstances will we submit to precensorship. I would rather take risks. This is one of our characteristics, that we have been prepared to take risks and it has landed us in trouble.'[114] He argued the same point with Coetzee, who was concerned that Ravan would not take on his second novel:

> As you will realise, censorship is a particularly raw point at
> present, with Jensma's second volume having been banned
> on the same day that you wrote. . . . Ravan's finances are still
> very tight, but I believe that we have little justification for
> our existence if we cannot take considered risks.[115]

In truth, though, Ravan was forced to turn down some titles. Criticised at the time for being afraid to publish, Randall admits now that he feared bannings – with good reason – and could not risk the already shaky finances of the press.

The effect of the 1976 Soweto Uprising was increased surveillance and clampdowns on opposition. The government set up the Schlebusch Commission to investigate the causes, but it extended this mandate to

---

[112] Nicol, 'Ravan flies out of the red'.
[113] Randall to Manganyi, 10 September 1975. PMA
[114] Nicol, 'Ravan flies out of the red'.
[115] Randall to Coetzee, 21 July 1975, 1998.8.1, Amazwi.

investigating cultural groups – including the Christian Institute. Thus, the consequences of state harassment were not only financial; being an oppositional publisher was dangerous. The security police and other agents of the state were extremely aggressive in their treatment of Ravan Press: authors and staff were harassed and monitored; books were regularly banned and confiscated; there were raids and vandalism, and even firebombing. Randall refers to these events regularly in his correspondence, citing 'court cases, visits from police and other unsavoury matters'.[116] This can be illustrated by the banning of *Confused Mhlaba*, a short play by Khayalethu Mqayisa. The Publications Committee argued that the work could adversely affect race relations, as the name 'Mhlaba', which can mean country, suggested that the author was depicting South Africa as confused.[117] In this case, Ravan lodged an appeal, arguing, 'It is important for the maintenance of good relations that one section should be allowed to express its grievances, whether real or imagined, and any attempt to stifle this could only lead to resentment.'[118] The security police, who searched his home, interrogated the author; he was threatened with physical harm; and his wife received anonymous phone calls claiming that her husband was having an affair. Similar tactics were used against Randall: his phone calls were monitored, his wife received anonymous tip-offs and his passport was confiscated. Randall describes the tension and fear: 'People we knew had been murdered, our house was vulnerable. We were very aware of security police monitoring and involvement.'[119] In September 1977, they heard the news of their former colleague Steve Biko's death in detention.

Just a month later, in October 1977, Randall himself was banned, along with Van Zyl and Naude, on charges relating to the Suppression of Communism Act. At least forty black leaders were detained in the same month, and eighteen organisations were declared unlawful. The Schlebusch Commission, accusing the CI of supporting 'violent change . . . regardless of the possibility that their actions might lead to the violent overthrow of the authority of the state', finally succeeded in closing it down.

---

[116] Randall to Coetzee, 11 January 1974, 1998.8.1, Amazwi.
[117] Randall, 'Banning of Confused Mhlaba'.
[118] Randall, 'Banning of Confused Mhlaba'. [119] Randall, interview.

Randall's banning meant he could no longer be involved with Ravan. For a time, Gill Berchowitz kept the Press afloat: 'For the months after Peter was banned, I had to figure things out by myself and by going to his house and asking him. His phone was tapped and he was under a huge amount of surveillance so I couldn't just call if something came up.'[120] She adds, 'During the time after the bannings, the security police regularly popped in, which was quite a challenge.'[121] Nadine Gordimer reflected, rather condescendingly:

> When I hear Jimmy Kruger talking of the dark plots of the 'revolutionaries' he has put away where they can do no harm, by banning them, and I think of my friend Peter Randall, living around the corner, the founder of a tiny, lively, publishing firm, whose sin of treason seems to have been that he published books that showed what the young black consciousness movements were thinking – poems, factual studies, and harmless not-very-good plays and stories that had no political significance whatever except to show, perhaps, how sadly most aspirant black writers lack education.[122]

Randall describes himself as 'an ordinary South African who detested the government policies and who sympathised with ordinary black South Africans'.[123] Berchowitz says, 'He was a radical in the most fundamental and down-to-earth way. He recognized the deadly effects of apartheid and the imperative to expose its effects on SA society through the best quality books in all fields that he could find and make available in affordable editions. He did this under tremendous stress.'[124] An author sympathised: 'for Peter it must have been shattering to see a publishing house he has so selflessly nurtured over these past years into the vital force it is, suddenly wrenched away. That it should go on is imperative.'[125] And go on it did: Randall had already been making plans to bring in a literary editor, Mike

---

[120] Berchowitz, email message. [121] Berchowitz, email message.
[122] Gordimer, quoted in Roberts, *No Cold Kitchen*, 395–6. [123] Randall, interview.
[124] Berchowitz, email message. [125] Nicol to Kirkwood, 2 November 1977. PMA

Kirkwood. Kirkwood wrote to the poet Mike Nicol: 'the State has zapped Peter and articles in the press have posted the question-mark against the future of Ravan. We go on: this is certainly my feeling, and I'm sure it's shared by everyone else connected with the outfit. Peter will be a tremendous loss. ... We'll just have to work like hell and keep the books coming.'[126]

3 Writing for Liberation

A New Vision

Mike Kirkwood was an accidental publisher. 'The whole thing landed in my lap,' he said, when asked if he would take over Ravan as a whole after Randall's banning.[127] Kirkwood was 'a severe Marxist critic of the white literary tradition, a distinctive scholarly product of the intellectual upheaval at the University of Natal in the 1970s'.[128] Born in the West Indies, he played an important role in supporting South African writing, as a lecturer in Natal and through the magazine *Bolt*, with Tony Morphet. Working on *Bolt* brought him into contact with writers' collectives around the country, and he had what he later called a *Eureka!* moment: 'If there are writers, there must be readers. How do we find them?' This gave him the idea to provide a platform: 'black writers were beginning to write for a different readership. They were starting to experiment with literary forms that would suit their urgent need to communicate – and they were looking to black readers.'[129]

When Kirkwood took the helm, he did not see himself as a publisher per se; 'I am trying as time goes by to understand what publishing is and can be in the cultural context I inhabit,'[130] he wrote to Mbulelo Mzamane, and later, 'I think that a publisher should always attempt to respond to as many cultural phenomena as possible. The essence of publishing is to be

---

[126] Kirkwood to Nicol, 27 October 1977. PMA
[127] Bryer, 'Publishing in the wake', 129.
[128] Breckenridge, 'Hopeless Entanglement'.
[129] Bryer, 'Publishing in the wake', 129.
[130] Kirkwood to M.V. Mzamane, 17 March 1980, PMA.

open.'[131] He aimed to continue Ravan's existing strengths – 'the socio-political, mainly academic analyses of our society, generally "pro-change" without a fixed ideological position; the need to survive financially – the occasional book that we do for commercial reasons'.[132] But, based on his own interests and the context of increasing radicalisation of literature in South Africa in the late 1970s, he also had a new mission: 'to embody the work of a writers' movement operating so-to-speak "behind the lines" of the erstwhile (and still formally) "dominant" culture in our country'. He went on to describe this publishing philosophy as follows:

> [I]ntellectually diverse – from the highly educated to the newly literate; a prevailing collective identity which includes within it some vulnerable and alienated life-experiences; a high degree of political commitment within the broad framework of black consciousness; needing urgently to set down the collectively perceived key experiences of the oppressed; exulting in the discovery of a potentially huge new audience with whom the writer feels at one; occasionally looking over the shoulder at those readers in the 'dominant' culture the 'dominated' writers used to address.[133]

Many of Kirkwood's ideas about publishing stemmed from the work of Walter Benjamin on storytelling and bearing witness. Benjamin argued that 'real stories' arose from a specific time and place, and the storyteller's own experiences: 'The storyteller takes what he tells from experience – his own or that reported by others. And he in turn makes it the experience of those who are listening to his tale.'[134] Given this idea of writing for a purpose, Kirkwood went on to formulate a mission of 'writing for liberation'.[135] He understood that writers had to balance their commitment to writing and their role in the struggle. But this confused many, with one writer asking:

---

[131] Schwartz, 'Letting the cats out of the bag', 11.
[132] Kirkwood to Mzamane, 17 March 1980, PMA.
[133] Kirkwood to Mzamane, 17 March 1980, PMA.   [134] Benjamin, 'The storyteller'.
[135] Kirkwood to Manaka, 30 September 1977, PMA

> Ravan's policy has always seemed more than a little ambig-
> uous to me. I have never been able to figure out whether
> they are truly interested in running a commercial publishing
> house or are only interested in promoting the so-called
> liberation struggle . . . is it the writing or the social change
> that is important? . . . Is it literary merit and commercial
> potential that is important or is it the other?[136]

Kirkwood's answer: the one wasn't possible without the other; storytelling and witness could not be dissociated: 'We don't mind if the books at first seem Utopian or provocative.'[137]

The key vehicle for storytelling was *Staffrider*. The idea for this magazine came from a meeting of minds between Kirkwood and Mothobi Mutloatse, a journalist and founding member of the banned black writers' group Medupe. Mutloatse floated the idea for a magazine, and he had a name for it: *Staffrider*.[138] A staffrider, Kirkwood later explained, is a 'mobile, disreputable bearer of tidings', implying 'a comparison between the liberties the staffrider took with the law and the liberties we wanted the magazine to take with the censorship system'.[139] This germ of an idea would set a new direction for Ravan Press and later lend its name to a new generation of writers. Kirkwood took the initiative for implementing this idea at Ravan and brought Mutloatse in as a non-executive director.

In January 1978, Kirkwood and Mutloatse sent out feelers to a broad network of writers' collectives across the country, informing them of plans for a new magazine: 'Basically the magazine is to be a bi-monthly outlet for groups of writers around the country who will select and edit their own contributions as well as distributing the magazine.'[140] Material flooded in. Disregarding Sipho Sepamla's warning – 'To edit a magazine aimed at a black

---

[136] Ebersohn to Kirkwood, 1977, PMA. [137] Bryer, 'Publishing in the wake'.
[138] Marilyn (Kirkwood) Honikman, interview with author, 23 May 2016; Mothobi Mutloatse, interview with author, 16 September 2019.
[139] Kirkwood, 'An informal discussion', 23.
[140] Kirkwood to James Matthews, 17 January 1978, PMA.

readership in this country is an exercise in futility'[141] – they encountered their first obstacle when the first issue of *Staffrider* was banned, after selling out the print run of 1 500 within the first week. They turned this to their advantage, however, using the pages of the magazine to describe their experiences with censorship: 'A poem is not a gun,' they argued, 'the untrammelled publication of new black writing helps rather than hinders the cause of peace.'[142]

While officially apolitical, the magazine was a forum in which political activity could be re-channelled into a cultural form. It was positioned as non-racial and committed to publishing writers from across the political spectrum – 'Douglas Livingstone of Durban and Mango Tshabangu of Jabavu could be side by side on the same page'[143] – although in the early years the Black Consciousness ideology was dominant.[144] Ivan Vladislavic, who later joined Ravan as an editor, links 'the journal's original self-editing format [to] the message of self-reliance integral to Black Consciousness ideology.'[145] Even 'the name chosen for the magazine and its mode of organisation indicated that its spiritual home was the black urban townships of South Africa and that most of its contributors would be drawn from the new and mainly young writers who live there.'[146] Matsemela Manaka would later describe the magazine as being as much a movement as a publication, while Penfold calls it 'a notorious cultural forum during the liberation struggle'.[147] Descriptions of *Staffrider* often employ such adjectives – urgent, defiant, confrontational, militant (even scruffy): 'From the outset, *Staffrider* flouted almost every decorum of sacerdotal authority. A fierce rebuttal of white poetic standards, the magazine paraded an aesthetics of calculated defiance and collectivity.'[148] Visually, this defiance was expressed in BCM-inspired imagery, chief among these being a raised fist and an emphasis on the black body, especially as expressed in the work of artists like Thami Mnyele, Fikile and Muziwakhe Nhlabatsi.[149]

---

[141] Sepamla, 'Note on New Classic', 83.
[142] Mike Kirkwood, Report on *Staffrider*, 1979, 1998.8.42.1, Amazwi.
[143] Breckenridge, 'Hopeless entanglement', 1255–6.
[144] Davis, *Voices of Justice*, 167–8. [145] Vladislavic & Oliphant, 'Prologue', ii.
[146] Kirkwood, Report on Staffrider. [147] Penfold, 'Black Consciousness'.
[148] McClintock, '*Azikwelwa*'. [149] Hill, *Iconography of Black Conciousness*.

Part of the mythology around *Staffrider* is that it was run as a collective, that editorial decisions were made by consensus and that there was little to no editing. An editorial in the first issue set out this policy:

> We hope that the work appearing in this magazine will be selected and edited as far as possible by the groups themselves. The magazine is prepared for publication by Ravan Press but has no editor or editorial board in the usual sense.[150]

And in a later issue:

> [E]ditorial control is vested in the writers as participants in a community-based group. Those who suggest that *Staffrider* should appoint an editor whose task is to impose "standards" on the magazine are expressing – consciously or unconsciously – an elitist view of art which cannot comprehend the new artistic energies released in the tumult of 1976 and after.[151]

Kirkwood consciously promoted this view of a *writer's* paper, with minimal editorial oversight, arguing, 'The magazine doesn't have a policy as such ... the magazine gets its flavour from the people who use it most and distribute it most – black writers.'[152] He believed that the content should be shaped by writers themselves, and not imposed from outside: 'The publisher seeking to operate in concert with a writers' movement is in a different position to the publisher who judges the work of individual manuscripts, rejecting or accepting in the name of the standards of a universal readership.'[153] Kirkwood thus criticised many existing literary journals, seeing their commitment to so-called aesthetic standards as a pretext for gatekeeping and exclusion.[154] The lack of an editorial board has led to some confusion about Ravan's role. For instance, Stephen Gray

---

[150] Editorial, *Staffrider* 1(1), 1978, 3.   [151] *Staffrider* 2(3) (1979): 58.

[152] Kirkwood to Wessel Ebersohn, 10 July 1978, PMA.

[153] Kirkwood to Mzamane, 1980, PMA.   [154] Kirkwood, 'The Colonizer'.

described *Staffrider* as being 'under Ravan's protection' in 1980,[155] while Njabulo Ndebele later described the magazine as taking 'advantage of the publishing capacity of Ravan Press'.[156] He went on: 'The magazine wanted to encourage this flowering of artistic activity by leaving editorial decisions to contributing art groups, as it articulated in its editorial policy.' When Wally Serote first wrote to *Staffrider* offering short stories around 1980, Jaki Seroke responded, pointing out that 'we don't have an editor as such.'[157] This laissez-faire approach to editing is characteristic of oppositional publishers: 'A democratic publication sacrifices professionalism so that all the voices, even the halting and poorly expressed, can be heard.'[158] And the writers responded well: 'Although there are far glossier magazines in South Africa, I find myself writing more and more for *Staffrider.*'[159]

This approach to editorial responsibility is reflected in the setting. Ravan had offices in an old house in central Johannesburg, 'practically the last house left in a neighbourhood of flats and hotels'.[160] There were a few separate offices and a large, shambolic common room. Staff meetings were often held on wooden benches in the backyard. Vladislavic describes the warehouse: 'This awkward space, which must have been meant for hay bales and harnesses, was crammed with books in teetering piles, *Muriel at Metropolitan*, *Call Me Not a Man*, *Dusklands* – the hardcover edition, which had not sold well – back issues of the Spro-cas reports and *Staffrider.*' He sketches a vivid scene:

> There were a dozen of us working at Ravan Press. The editors – the other two were Mike Kirkwood and Kevin French – sat together in a single room, two desks on either side, facing one another across a narrow channel. We talked and joked, overheard one another's telephone conversations, edited and argued. Frequently we rearranged the

---

[155] Gray, 'The year that was', 156. [156] Ndebele, 'The Writers' Movement'.

[157] Serote to Ravan, 15 January 1980. PMA

[158] McMillian, *Smoking Typewriters*, 25.

[159] Rive interview, in Lindfors, ed. *Africa Talks Back*, 337.

[160] Vladislavic, 'Staffrider'.

schedule. We worked hard too, as the publishing record
shows. We were harassed by impatient authors and the
security police.[161]

Collective production also meant cheaper production. The staff were encouraged to learn the basics of editing, design and layout. Desktop publishing
technology was becoming more accessible, and Kirkwood bought a Wang
typesetting machine. Merle Stoltenkamp, Dorothy Wheeler and Anne
Robertson were trained to use this, to get the books out quickly – the aim
being to sell as many copies as possible before a potential banning.[162] Mike's
wife, Marilyn, was drafted to help with the sales and marketing, at first with
no salary. Former students of Mike's, such as Andy Mason, were brought in,
along with Biddy Crewe and Joyce Ozynski. A number of authors were also
employed and were encouraged to think of themselves as part of the team,
doing the 'dirty work'.[163] Thus, 'Writers acted as editors; illustrators acted as
critics; photographers acted as distributors, and the publishers acted as
litigants publicly defending their magazine against the encroaching censorship of the Publications Directorate.'[164] From 1979, there was on-the-job
training for writers like Matsemela Manaka and Jaki Seroke, brought in to
work on *Staffrider* and coordinate black writers. Manaka found that the
'unusually democratic' structure at Ravan provided valuable experience:
'His work was partly that of a public relations manager; he developed an
informal distribution network based on the notion that writers should involve
themselves in the distribution of their work (an idea which finally had to be
acknowledged as a failure).'[165] With Seroke, he also conducted writers'
workshops and helped establish writers' groups. Employees 'felt really connected and important' and of immediate relevance: 'I never for a day thought
what I was doing didn't have a purpose,' says Vladislavic.[166] Seroke describes
a similar sense of purpose.

---

[161] Vladislavic, 'A vivid voice'. [162] Honikman, interview.

[163] 'Ravan Press' to Friedman, 26 September 1986. PMA

[164] Keaney, 'From the Sophiatown shebeens', 279.

[165] Davis, *Voices of Justice*, 167–8; also Kirkwood, 'An informal discussion', 24.

[166] In O'Toole, 'Uncommon criticism'.

In addition, writers were encouraged to drop in at the office, which doubled as a meeting place, providing a material context for writers, artists and photographers to share ideas – a rare space in the segregated apartheid landscape. Meetings for PEN (Johannesburg) were also often held at the office. This branch was established in 1978 to bring together the mostly white writers' guild and township writing collectives, and the membership criteria were changed to become more inclusive. Both established writers such as Nadine Gordimer and Lionel Abrahams and emerging writers attended the meetings. As Kirkwood pointed out,

> There is of course no <u>direct</u> connection between the magazine and the P.E.N. centre which was formed last year. But most of the 100+ writers who have appeared in *Staffrider* are associate members or full members of P.E.N. The obvious point of contact is the groups. The P.E.N. centre acts as a co-ordinator for the groups (workshops, readings, cases of harassment, care of families of imprisoned writers, etc) just as *Staffrider* co-ordinates the publishing end of the writing.[167]

This kind of concrete support for writers was very significant in a period of state-sponsored oppression.

The staff also enjoyed the energy of many people calling at the office; Kirkwood found it 'much easier to sit down and talk to them than to write lengthy criticism',[168] which perhaps explains his notoriously slow responses to correspondence. Seroke says of Kirkwood, 'Mike was a broad-minded person and able to deal with good writers. I think he had a gift of dealing with people from different backgrounds, and making them at ease.'[169] This community building, drawing together previously scattered and isolated writers' groups, and making them more cohesive, is key to Ravan's work, although it has been overshadowed somewhat by Kirkwood's larger-than-life personality: 'What *Staffrider* had initiated was essentially a dialectical

---

[167] Kirkwood, 'Report on Staffrider'.
[168] Kirkwood, 'An informal discussion', 22, 24.
[169] Jaki Seroke, interview with author, 16 October 2019.

process: it printed work emanating from writers' groups across the country, but its own very existence was becoming a guiding force in establishing such groups.'[170] The larger movement was thus reflected in collective production – no publication was the outcome of a single person's work.

This was clearly not a publisher staffed by professionals; they were activists first and publishers second. The lack of structures has led to a general perception of lower quality, and a lack of concern for literary standards. Various commentators have criticised *Staffrider*'s apparent lack of editing and uneven quality. Ursula Barnett describes 'the impression that here gathers a crowd of people who have been waiting to release a flood of pent-up emotions in words. *Staffrider* opened the sluice-gates and out it poured, good bad and indifferent. . . . There is little attempt to edit, even where necessary.'[171] Even some of the authors were disappointed in the quality of the writers; Mbulelo Mzamane, for one, was criticised for having a stiff, canonical notion of standards. But this isn't the whole story. The actual publishing practice, although amateurish at times, shows an abiding interest in review and editing, and good design. *Staffrider*'s 'mosaic-like layout' illustrates this point.[172] Without any background in typesetting, Kirkwood laid out the first issue at home: he physically cut out the headings and text and pasted them over the pages of an issue of *Time*, using the established magazine as a template.[173] The resulting grid-like structure worked well in unifying the disparate submissions of text and image, and the masthead remained the same throughout the magazine's existence.

More significantly, in sharp contrast to perceptions, material *was* carefully sifted and edited by the small editorial group. As Andries Oliphant has pointed out, 'submissions were edited by a relatively permanent editorial and production staff at Ravan Press.'[174] In the archives, the surviving original manuscripts bear the marks of a great deal of interventionist editing – especially in Kirkwood's distinctive handwriting. For instance, the manuscript for Shabbir Banoobhai's poems, *Shadows of a Sun-Darkened Land* (1984), contains many marginal comments: 'It's done now'; 'Shabbir,

---

[170] Davis, *Voices of Justice*, 167–8.   [171] Barnett, *Vision of Order*, 38.

[172] Vaughan, 'Staffrider and Directions', 198.   [173] Honikman, interview.

[174] Oliphant, 'Staffrider Magazine and Popular History', 359.

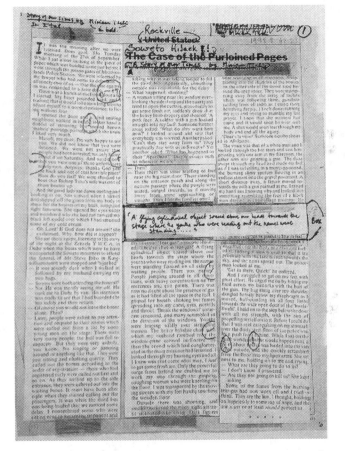

The paste-up layout of Staffrider, volume 1 (Source: Amazwi)

I think you should leave this one out'; 'This may be the best poem you've done.'[175] Banoobhai called Kirkwood a 'passionate critic of my poems' and valued his editing.[176] Similarly, the children's author Marguerite Poland

---

[175] Notes on manuscript, 1998.8.38, Amazwi.   [176] Banoobhai, personal blog.

described her relationship: 'I am also very lucky that I have such a superb editor in Mike Kirkwood of Ravan Press. When Mike has read the manuscript he gives me constructive criticism.'[177] Kirkwood described his editing as highlighting issues – 'All you can do is point, and try and explain what you felt was wrong'[178] – but it was far more substantive and developmental.

More selection also became inevitable as an 'avalanche of material' came in:

> Already the print is packed too tight for comfortable reading, and the typesetting bill on *Staffrider* is considerable. One solution would be to become selective. I feel, though, that this would destroy the . . . characteristic of the mag – its function as an accessible public forum for writers of diverse backgrounds, variously oriented, variously expressed.[179]

Chris van Wyk was appointed editor in 1982 and 'gave voice to a more critical, less racially exclusive position and an increasing concern with aesthetic issues'.[180] It has been suggested that his editorship coincided with a shift in editorial policy, and that he insisted on 'a system of literary merit',[181] but in fact the magazine – like the books – was always subject to both selection and editing. After 1982, though, the 'initial and very fertile momentum' slowed. Kirkwood wrote to Kunene, 'I think we need to define a new phase in "cultural reconstruction". . . . I hope that *Staffrider* can play its part in beginning to develop authentic new values.'[182]

'The Best in Black Writing Today'

The demand for new writing led to more books being published, especially by young black writers. Kirkwood's and Mutloatse's contacts and those of the writers considerably enlarged the existing networks forged by Spro-cas.

---

[177] 'Appeal gives rise to skill', *Eastern Province Herald*, 24 May 1982.
[178] Kirkwood to Gwala, January 1984, PMA.
[179] Kirkwood to Coetzee, 1978, PMA.
[180] Van Wyk, 'Staffrider and the Politics of Culture', 166.
[181] Van Wyk, 'Staffrider and the Politics of Culture', 166.
[182] Kirkwood to Daniel Kunene, 18 August 1983, PMA.

Kirkwood recalls Matsemela Manaka walking into the office, 'coming not as an individual but carrying with him, as it were, a whole group of writers'.[183] The writer Rose Zwi, working as an editor at Ravan, described the late 1970s:

> It was an extraordinary era. Poems, stories and plays came flooding in to Ravan from writers' groups throughout the country. They were written in pen or pencil, on pages torn from scrapbooks, or on the back of cigarette boxes. Much of this writing was far from literate, let alone literary – the effects of Bantu Education had taken a heavy toll. But they all gave an insight into the depth of suffering endured by the black people. Established writers also sent in poems and stories. At poetry readings in the townships, writers of all races read their work to a sometimes puzzled audience. And Ingoapele Madingoale strode the boards to the sound of drums, declaiming, 'Africa my beginning, and Africa my ending.'[184]

Madingoale's performance poem was published in 1979, with cover artwork by Fikile. It was already well known to the people of Soweto: 'Of all the oral poems of this period, this long work has made the deepest sustained impact. In 1978 it was recited at a mass meeting to commemorate the Soweto Uprising, and frequent performances have made fragments of the poem a part of popular memory.'[185] Seroke recalls, however, that the work needed considerable repackaging to make it suitable for publication, as it was meant for performance rather than reading.[186] Unsurprisingly for a book described as 'a litany of resistance',[187] it was banned after three weeks. In that time, it had already sold around 2 000 copies.

While *Staffrider* has mostly been studied on its own, it both fed into and was sustained by the publishing of books, acting as a 'nursery' for the literary publishing programme. Writers tended to first contribute to *Staffrider*, and the

---

[183] Kirkwood, 'An informal discussion', 22–31. The title of this section comes from an advertisement in *Frontline*, October 1982, PMA.

[184] Zwi, 'In conversation'. [185] Kirkwood, 'Report on Staffrider'.

[186] Seroke, interview. [187] Kirkwood to Rex Collings, 5 September 1979, PMA.

books were aimed at a similar readership. Mtutuzeli Matshoba followed this pattern:

> [A]s we started to publish Matshoba in *Staffrider* we quickly became aware that there might be the prospect of a book at the end of the line, and we were able, in fact, to cut costs by using the original typesetting, playing it out in book format. This is something that we try to do: see writers who appear in the magazine as people who may well be producing books in the near future.[188]

Moreover:

> In its early days *Staffrider* attracted a large readership, especially in the black townships, and Matshoba was easily the most prominent, and most imitated, of its fiction writers. He was thus, for a time, possibly the most influential fiction writer in South Africa: He has . . . become identified with the magazine, and this association is not gratuitous.[189]

Kirkwood saw Matshoba as embodying his conception of a storyteller: 'I confess that I find it difficult, as I read Matshoba's stories, not to see him in front of me.'[190] The manuscript for *Call Me Not A Man* is covered in notes and editorial comments, adjusting the style, correcting the language, deleting sections and in some cases inserting whole paragraphs. This is particularly striking because Kirkwood was criticised for rushing the book into print, without editorial intervention:

> Your arguments for publishing *Call Me Not* as it stands, looked at from your point of view, are quite compelling but I'm afraid they're not nearly as convincing to me. Hell, Mike, you missed a golden opportunity of showing these

---

[188] Kirkwood, 'An informal discussion'. [189] MacKenzie, 'Njabulo Ndebele', 30.
[190] Introduction to Mzamane, ed. *Hungry Flames*, xxiii.

boys, some of whom are growing to be extremely unself-
critical, how a writer, through the tyranny of revolution, can
polish and improve his work.[191]

Mzamane accepted that 'rawer' versions of writing could appear in *Staffrider*
but argued that they needed more polishing before appearing in book form.
Writers 'need an enlightened watchdog and a guiding hand', and 'Mtutuzeli
never received the kind of assistance he is entitled to receive from his
publishing house.' Yet the book was very favourably received: Alan Paton
called the collection the 'best South African short stories I have read for a long
time,' while the academic David Maughan Brown found this 'a landmark in
the development of South African short-story writing'.[192] Matshoba's next
work, *Seeds of War*, was banned for showing 'militant confrontation with the
authorities . . . calculated to cause racial friction'.[193] Reviewers saw the work
as 'a shocking, deeply moving piece of contemporary history, beautifully
written'.[194] A number of other significant works were also banned, especially
those that dealt directly with political issues, such as Christopher Hope's
A Separate Development and Miriam Tlali's second novel, *Amandla!* This does
not imply, however, that all of the work was political.

Ravan also responded to the growing black 'theatre of the dispossessed',
with the Ravan Playscripts series. Cheaply produced to reach a broader
audience, these included Zakes Mda's award-winning *We Shall Sing for the
Fatherland*, as well as Ronnie Govender's *The Lahnee's Pleasure* and
Matsemela Manaka's indictment of migrant labour conditions in *Egoli*.[195]
Egoli was banned, but it was also voted 'Best Play of the Year' in London in
1982. Writing to playwright Daniel Kunene, Kirkwood complained, 'Plays
are hell to publish, as you know.'[196] Similarly, poetry could be difficult. The
Staffrider network brought in many poems, the best of which were collected

[191] Mzamane to Kirkwood, 6 May 1980, PMA.
[192] Sole, 'Political fiction', 101–21.
[193] Directorate of Publications report, P83/3/119, PMA.
[194] John Eppel, Review, *Sunday Tribune*, 27 February 1983, PMA.
[195] Chapman, 'The year that was (1981)', 170–1.
[196] Kirkwood to Kunene, 3 May 1984, PMA.

in book form. The early 1980s saw collections by poets like Mafika Gwala, Achmat Dangor and Modikwe Dikobe. Jeremy Cronin's poetry collection, *Inside*, reflected on his years as a political prisoner and represented an attempt 'to find a language that is a part of and makes him part of the emergent national culture'.[197] Similar issues of language and identity emerged in the titling of an anthology of black South African poetry, as Njabulo Ndebele objected to the working title *Ask Any Black Man*:

> The suggested title really represents no conceptual advance on *To Whom It May Concern*, a title published by Donker in 1973. So we are talking of an interval of almost ten years! Surely much has happened in South Africa during this interval. At that time, when *To Whom It May Concern* was published, we were being revealed to White South Africa. . . . The onus was on us to prove our humanity . . . to show that there was something behind the statistic. The liberal publisher was really bringing us out to dance. . . . Who should ask any black man? Surely not another African.[198]

The anthology was renamed *The Return of the Amasi Bird*. Ndebele was a significant influence on Ravan, serving as a trustee, writing for *Staffrider* and publishing books. His *Fools and Other Stories* won the 1984 Noma Award, and a Longman Drumbeats edition appeared in the United Kingdom in 1985.

Due to the intervention of Marilyn Kirkwood, Ravan also branched into less familiar areas of children's books and schoolbooks, with the unexpected success of Marguerite Poland's prizewinning *The Mantis and the Moon*. Isobel Randall, Peter's wife and a successful author, was brought in to work on the growing list, and she teamed up with Gerald de Villiers of Hodder & Stoughton Educational.[199] One of their titles, *Our*

---

[197]   *First Impressions*, 1(1) (1984), 2, PMA.

[198]   Ndebele, 'Life-sustaining poetry', 44–5.

[199]   Marilyn Kirkwood and Isobel Randall both deserve more attention and more credit for their behind the scenes work at Ravan – a story which will have to be told elsewhere.

Village Bus (by Maria Mabetoa and illustrated by Mzwakhe), was one of the first picture books written and illustrated by black South Africans. It was hoped that such books would be prescribed in large quantities for schools and generate a profit to fund less lucrative titles, but this was only partially successful. A very different sort of children's book was *Two Dogs and Freedom*, a facsimile reproduction of children's work compiled by the Open School, an alternative education project for black youth in the townships. It is a striking depiction of apartheid's violence and was banned in August 1986.[200] Ravan argued, 'The book is not political. It is just a reflection of the reality the children perceive in a township occupied by soldiers and police.'[201]

A Concern with Everyday Life

Ravan's fiction aimed to speak directly to the reader, and the same was true of its non-fiction. Most studies of Ravan emphasise the literary, but non-fiction in fact made up more than half the list. These titles fit well with Kirkwood's vision, as they link storytelling and popular history. The books – often by radical white academics – made a deliberate attempt to critique society. The writing of history was seen as particularly important: 'The recovery and utilisation of cultural resources buried by the past ... is a task for the cultural activist as much as the scholar.'[202] In this effort, Ravan was joined by the History Workshop at Witwatersrand University. The workshop was launched in 1978 'to develop a history which, far from being either boring or propagandistic, can be translated readily into other idioms and media' and which can 'resonate with the lives of ordinary people'.[203] It aimed to produce short, accessible books to popularise history, and to establish a relationship with an audience of 'black and white working people, youth, teachers, students, rural dwellers, and the unemployed, whose voices were being increasingly heard in the context of growing trade unionism, populism,

---

[200] Excerpt from Judgement from Publications Appeal Board, PMA.
[201] 'Essays by children banned', PMA.
[202] Kirkwood, 'Literature and Popular Culture', 658.
[203] Bozzoli, 'Town and Countryside', 1.

and nationalism'.[204] Kirkwood explained: 'The latest drive has been to remind high school and campus students of their history not as interpreted by the writers of their textbooks, but by people with alternative perspectives.'[205] This was history from below – 'from the lower terrain of the township house, the mine compound or the farm hut'[206] – and aimed at a working-class audience.[207]

Some very influential histories were published in this period, including work by Phil Bonner, Belinda Bozzoli, Peter Delius, Dan O'Meara and Jeff Guy. Some contained experiments with genre: *Town and Countryside*, for instance, included Modikwe Dikobe's poem, *Dispossessed*, alongside more conventional historical writing. These were modestly profitable books: Charles van Onselen's series of *Studies in the Social and Economic History of the Witwatersrand, 1886–1914* all sold more than 1 000 copies. Luli Callinicos points out that this popularity was linked to the style of the books: 'In South Africa, popular history must be judged as much by its accessibility as by its content since the readership often has little formal education, and speaks English as a second or third language.'[208] Her title, *Working Life*, won the Noma Award in 1988 and was cited as a 'unique exercise in writing and presenting history to a popular audience ... produced in close discussion with workers themselves, giving it special immediacy and relevance'.[209] A golden thread running through these works was the history of resistance, which could be traced back as far as Sol. T. Plaatje's *Native Life in South Africa*, which Ravan reprinted in 1982.

These works found traction in a context in which the influence of Black Consciousness was waning, and the labour movement and United Democratic Front were on the rise.[210] Ravan sought co-publications with

---

[204] Bozzoli, 'Intellectuals, Audiences and Histories'.

[205] Kirkwood to Gwala, 18 January 1984, PMA.

[206] Review of Peter Delius, *The Land Belongs to Us*, PMA.

[207] Callinicos, 'Popular History in the Eighties'.

[208] Callinicos, 'Popular History in the Eighties', 291.

[209] Noma Award jury citation, 1988.

[210] The United Democratic Front was a non-racial coalition of civil society and workers' organisations, formed while the ANC was still banned.

trade unions to reach a wider audience and to further 'the possible supportive role this publishing house can play towards the labor movement'.[211] Kevin French was particularly active, developing a proposal for worker publications to be distributed as widely as possible, using the trade unions – 'a distribution network which does not rely solely on the commodity market'.[212] The series was complemented by a working class component in *Staffrider*, with short articles by workers themselves. For instance, *Ilanga Lizophumelo Abasebenzi* is the story of Mandlenkhosi Makhoba, a shop steward, assisted by his friend Paul Stewart, while worker poet Alfred Qabula produced a series of auto-biographical poems. Stewart summed up the approach:

> Now the Ravan Worker Series is taking us a step forward. The aim of this series is to publish stories *by* workers, *for* workers, to give the *workers'* point of view. We think this is important because of the leading role of the workers in the struggle for a new South Africa. In this series we hope to publish stories by workers from different industries, regions, unions and races so that a Cape Town worker can know the story of a metal worker on the East Rand, and a Durban worker can hear the Cape Town workers' story and so on.[213]

In these titles, the authors try to speak directly to their readers and foster a rapport with them. This stylistic choice was carefully retained through the editing, as a review in *The Star* notes approvingly: 'This publication is effective because the writer's voice is authentic. The series could become powerful if this authenticity is continued. If stories like this can be made available to everybody it will help win the reform for the workers and praise for the publishers which is rightfully theirs.'[214]

One review of *Ilanga* was accompanied by an advertisement for the *Read Well* and *Write Well* books, aimed at teachers. SACHED's

---

[211] Kevin French to Alec Erwin, 24 January 1984. PMA

[212] Kevin French, press release for *Ilanga*, July 1984. PMA

[213] Paul Stewart, notes for launch of *Ilanga*, 14 July 1984, PMA.

[214] 'Take your story to the people', *The Star*, 25 September 1984.

Books for Workers (Source: South African History Online)

Publishing Project collaborated with Ravan to produce alternative, more balanced educational material beginning in 1984. *Read Well* and *Write Well* aimed to provide 'creative challenges to the constraints of English second language learning and teaching'.[215] These titles were reprinted in the thousands and sold well, albeit at a very low price. They were thus not particularly profitable, as handwritten costings show: 'the gain can only be seen as a recoupment of the loss incurred on the first run and therefore in real terms this publication is running on break even only if all copies of the second run are sold.'[216] Later titles, including *The Right to Learn*, *Working Women* and *The Cell*, a biology workbook, were more profitable and regularly reprinted. But the relationship with SACHED was never smooth, as the Ravan staff believed they were being treated as mere printers rather than partners.

Titles for adult literacy classes were driven by similar motives, to make education more accessible, especially to newly literate adults. *I am Anna* by Isobel Randall was an English workbook based on a character called Anna, a 'typical' domestic worker, while Mary McKeever's *Thula Baba: An adult literacy reader* was produced anonymously, to give the impression that it was written by an 'ordinary' adult learner. These are relatively problematic titles, in that they were written by white women for a black audience but attempted to disguise their origins. This was standard practice for many educational publishers, but not a comfortable fit for Ravan. For some of these titles, it could be asked whether Ravan was trying to reach a lucrative market without taking into account its traditional readership – moving away from the ethos of writing for liberation.

Circulation and Audiences

The work of a storyteller involves an audience – 'the community to which the storyteller explicitly or implicitly refers'.[217] The readership for oppositional

---

[215] *First Impressions*, 1(3) (1984), PMA.

[216] 'Report on Co-publication Costs with SACHED Trust', 7 September 1985, PMA.

[217] Kirkwood, 'Literature and popular culture', 670.

publishers is often as politically defined as the publishers themselves. Ravan's audience was both local and international, mostly those who supported the struggle against apartheid. With censorship applied post-publication, 'books were banned after they were already in the marketplace.'[218] This intervention directly affected publishers at the stage of distribution and bookselling, precisely the link in the publishing value chain where they were weakest. To circumvent mainstream distribution as well as censorship, direct sales were sometimes used. Nadine Gordimer noted: 'The general idea is that it is better to have the books ship in quietly and sell modestly than to be unable to sell at all. If the book is subsequently banned, the author has the satisfaction of knowing that at least it has some chance to be read, if not widely.'[219] Ravan's aim was also to 'bypass the white-controlled book trade, which focused on bookshop sales in the white city and the apartheid education market, by reaching out directly to a mass, black readership in the townships'.[220] Kirkwood spoke passionately of reaching this audience, asking, 'Is it possible for writers in a ghetto community to reach a readership in that community? Is it possible for those communities to link up in a wider network of distribution?'[221] This market was very price sensitive, and so the books needed to be kept as affordable as possible: 'Because this is a grass-roots readership, we assume that it can't easily afford more than about R3,50 for a book.'[222] Moreover, this market had to be reached directly. In an interview in 1980, Kirkwood noted, '[t]he whole black readership in this country operates largely outside the normal channels of bookshops. ... So we use non-commercial outlets, outlets that derive from the writers' groups that we publish.'[223] To reach this audience, Ravan employed an informal 'salesman army', as Chris van Wyk describes:

> So these writer's groups would come and submit their poems and short stories, and then we'd phone them, when

---

[218] Matteau, 'Readership for banned literature', 83.

[219] De Lange, *Muzzled Muse*, 75.   [220] McDonald, *Literature Police*, 323.

[221] Kirkwood to Anne Walmsley, 17 October 1984, PMA.

[222] Kirkwood, 'Informal discussion', 28.

[223] Kirkwood, 'Informal discussion', 25–6.

Staffrider came from the printers. And they take copies, hundred copies here, twenty copies there, sixty copies there, and take them to their various writers' groups, and that's how it got disseminated around the country. I remember when I was working at *Staffrider*, there were vendors, they were actually like hawkers who came to buy books and *Staffrider* magazines in our office, and they went and stood on the pavement, put them on a blanket on the pavement or in cardboard boxes in the pavement, and sold these books from there. Some would sell them in the train, walking up and down in the train selling them.[224]

Based on this distribution pattern, Kirkwood estimated that between 80 per cent and 90 per cent went to the townships, although he thought that *Staffrider* still had a long way to go in terms of reaching potential readers.[225] In addition, the writers' movements helped foster a sense of connection to their readers. Ravan also encouraged public dialogue through events such as book launches and discussions. These launches were often informal, although serious affairs, with cheap wine and home-made tomato sandwiches. A launch, Kirkwood explained, 'is not a "prestige" function. It is the occasion of a dialogue between the writer and such reviewers, "media people", scholars, etc, as we can prevail on to respond to the book. There is no ceremony at all, and the publisher is simply the "hidden hand" producing a situation in which writers and a first circle of readers converse.'[226]

It could be argued, however, that Ravan was more successful in promoting black *writers* than reaching black *readers*. Oliphant, for one, cautions against seeing a black, 'mass' audience as necessarily large: 'For oppositional publishers concerned with reaching the oppressed, this market has since the penetration of literacy on this sub-continent, been relatively small.'[227]

---

[224] Matteau, 'Readership for banned literature', 160.
[225] Kirkwood, 'Report on Staffrider'.
[226] Kirkwood to Mobbs Moberly, 22 February 1984, PMA.
[227] Oliphant, 'South African publishers', 69.

Because of the direct sales method, 'It is difficult to discern how a wider audience of township dwellers not directly involved in the creation and distribution of *Staffrider* received the magazine.'[228] In addition, over time, informal sales became less effective, with some distributors not paying Ravan their share of the revenue, and others being harassed by the security police. More books were channelled to formal booksellers, and Marilyn had some success in selling to the CNA chain. As much as Kirkwood may have tried to deny this, arguing that the black writers were addressing 'a new readership – an African readership,'[229] the white audience was more significant in terms of sales. Lewis Nkosi has argued, 'for the black writer the kind of cross-border reader implied may be none other than the white South African reader' – and that this might apply 'even in the case of such valorised "township" texts as [those of] Mtutuzeli Matshoba'.[230] The writer Sipho Sepamla lamented: 'There are very few people who buy books by black writers. ... Unfortunately, it is true that most of the readers are white, so we're caught up in a very ironic situation because although we claim we are not writing for Whitey, we find that Whitey is the one who reads our works.'[231] Similarly, Jane Watts accepts that while protest writing found 'enthusiastic supporters among the entire literate black population, whose indignation and resentment it voiced,' it was 'directed mainly at a white readership'.[232]

The use of English inevitably added to this gap, but it enabled an overseas market. Kirkwood described Ravan's international readership as important, but not substantial – 'I wouldn't think it's more than 500 copies.'[233] In contrast, David Philip prioritised the international market, as the publishing house 'did not intend to limit [itself] to the small reading market of Southern Africa'.[234] This is borne out by the attention paid by the Philips to developing co-publishing and licensing links. However, external networks became increasingly important to Ravan as it battled to find sufficient funds and

---

[228] Keaney, 'From the Sophiatown Shebeens', 282.

[229] Schwartz, 'Letting the cats out of the bag', 11.

[230] Nkosi, 'Constructing the "Cross-Border" Reader', 45–6.

[231] In Brummer, *Processed World*.

[232] Watts, *Black Writers from South Africa*, 29.

[233] Kirkwood, 'Informal discussion', 26.   [234] Essery, 'Impact of Politics', 20.

bypass bannings. The initial impetus appears to have come from Rex Collings, who approached Ravan in the late 1970s to discuss co-publications. Collings, who had previously established the Three Crowns imprint for Oxford University Press to promote African writing, used his own imprint as a means to get more African writers into print and into the UK market. Trying to get books into other African countries was a more difficult task, even after the Zimbabwe International Book Fair was established in 1983.

One of Kirkwood's notebooks from the Frankfurt Book Fair survives and includes detailed notes on meetings with a wide range of publishers – Secker & Warburg (J.M. Coetzee's publishers), Harvest Press, Zed Press, Heinemann Educational Books, and publishers seeking translation rights – as well as distributors such as Third World Publications and Ohio University Press. Kirkwood met with Heinemann, and in particular James Currey, at Frankfurt in 1979, and agreed to offer an exclusive first option on new titles. (In practice, titles often had to be offered to Longman as well, depending on the author's preference.) The first Ravan/Heinemann book under this agreement was the anthology *Forced Landing*, edited by Mothobi Mutloatse, which was briefly banned in South Africa. Along with its successor, *Reconstruction*, *Forced Landing* was co-published and translated into German, French and Dutch. Similarly, Serote's *To Every Birth Its Blood* was sub-licensed to Heinemann, Longman picked up Matshoba's *Call Me Not a Man* for the Drumbeat series, and Mphahlele's *Chirundu* was published in America.

An example of the kind of reach and visibility generated by such co-publishing agreements has been described by Julie Frederikse, for her work *None but Ourselves: Masses vs media in the making of Zimbabwe*. Ravan originated the title, with a UK edition managed by James Currey for Heinemann. In the United States, Viking-Penguin was ambivalent about the market, but the editorial director wrote, 'This is an extraordinary book – it seems to me quite unique. As you can imagine, it won't be easy selling this book in America, but we'd like to give it a whirl.' As it happened, the US edition sold out. What is perhaps unique is that Penguin and Heinemann were persuaded to buy books printed in Harare, along with those printed for Ravan and the Zimbabwe Publishing House – a considerable saving over a combined print run of around 20 000 copies. As Frederikse notes, 'Heinemann's imprint already had "London Ibadan Nairobi" on the spine, but it was a first for Penguin to receive books printed in Africa.'[235] Subsidiary rights for the title were also sold, with an audiovisual show and a documentary broadcast on US public radio. Moreover, some of the images were re-used by other liberation movements.

Kirkwood later grew more disillusioned with the larger British publishers, warning an author, 'Don't be surprised to see AWS agents courting SKOTAVILLE and DONKER and RAVAN in an effort to spread their market monopoly style.'[236] He also felt despondent at a number of writers using Ravan as a springboard, electing for international publication once they had made a name for themselves. Mike Nicol recalls Kirkwood sitting behind his untidy desk: 'I sat down and he held up some pages from the manuscript he was reading and said, "You know this would make us a fortune but it's been sold to Gollancz in the UK. And I can't blame the author at all. I would've done the same."'[237] Kirkwood was referring to Wessel Ebersohn's first thriller *A Lonely Place to Die*, which went on to be published in fourteen countries. But even these authors valued their connection with Ravan and continued to advocate for a South African edition. For instance, Chabani Manganyi offered his biography of Es'kia Mphahlele, *Exiles and Homecomings*, to Ravan in 1983: 'You as my publisher of long standing deserve preferential consideration even though I would think your own commitments may dictate that other publishers such as Faber (Zeke's publisher as well) be approached.'[238] Similarly, Tom Lodge wrote to his British publisher, Longman: 'I would like to emphasise how much I value the Ravan connection; as the South African publishers of my first book they have been enthusiastic and supportive.'[239]

South Africa's two Nobel Prize laureates for literature, Nadine Gordimer and J.M. Coetzee, also kept local editions with Ravan. Gordimer published *The Black Interpreters* with Ravan in 1973 and ensured that her later novel *July's People* was co-published by Ravan and the small Afrikaans alternative

---

[235] Frederikse, 'Author's Reflections'.

[236] Kirkwood to Gwala, January 1984, PMA.

[237] Mike Nicol, 'A chat with Wessel Ebersohn'.

[238] Chabani Manganyi to Kirkwood, 24 April 1981, PMA.

[239] Tom Lodge to Chris Harrison, 11 July 1990, PMA.

publisher Taurus. This was intended as 'a gesture of support to the publishers who have done the most to withstand censorship'.[240] Ampie Coetzee of Taurus suggested that Gordimer's support showed that she 'wanted to be associated with our active protest', and that 'support from a writer and intellectual activist of her standing could only strengthen our little attempts at subversion.' Thereafter, Taurus would publish – jointly, either with Ravan or David Philip, after Kirkwood fell out with Gordimer – *Something Out There* (1984), *The Essential Gesture* (1988) and *My Son's Story* (1990). The collaboration was not necessarily lucrative; a note and royalty statement from Ampie Coetzee in September 1985 records just fourteen copies sold over the previous six months, and the wry comment, 'A very small cheque for Nadine! We don't sell dat book veddy well.'[241] Ravan sold around 200 copies in the same period.

Coetzee had published his debut, *Dusklands*, with Ravan in 1974; although he then switched to Secker & Warburg as his primary publisher, he too retained a close relationship.[242] He reassured the Press: 'Ravan will always have my fullest support for what it is trying to achieve.'[243] For specific titles, he negotiated the rights individually, and it seems at first his loyalty overrode his commercial instincts:

> I have thought at length about the question of who should sell MICHAEL K in South Africa. ... I must believe that Heinemann could do a good job of marketing the book here, probably a better job than Ravan Press, which is a smaller organization. However, as you know, I have been associated with Ravan since 1974 and owe them a certain debt. Furthermore I do believe they are filling a place in South African publishing that, by the nature of things, could not be filled by an overseas concern. So, giving full weight to the most persuasive arguments of the Heinemann people, and in full awareness that it is up to you alone to make the final

[240] Oliphant, *Celebrating Nadine Gordimer*.
[241] Ampie Coetzee to Kirkwood, 19 September 1985, PMA.
[242] Wittenberg, 'Taint of the Censor'.
[243] Coetzee to Marilyn Kirkwood, 5 March 1981, PMA.

decision, I must request that you consider giving the South
African rights to Ravan.[244]

Secker noted that he moved into 'another league' after his Booker Prize win,
and his manuscripts became unaffordable for Ravan. In spite of its inability
to compete with the larger multinational publishers, it was Ravan that
published these titles and ensured that they circulated throughout South
Africa – even in the face of stiff opposition.

4 A Balancing Act

Collective Organisation

Running Ravan Press involved balancing competing pressures. Internal
pressures stemmed from attempts to function as a collective and ongoing
struggles for funding. The publishing list would grow and shrink as a result,
and the time taken to produce a book could vary enormously. The Press
could also not escape its milieu: the harsh segregation enforced by apartheid
legislation created friction between black and white, even among people
ostensibly working towards the same goal. And all of this took place amidst
relentless pressure from the state and its security apparatus, monitoring,
harassing and restricting the staff at every turn.

From the very beginning, funding was an issue, and financial management was not Kirkwood's strong suit. Soon after taking over at Ravan, he
took a crash course in bookkeeping: 'For a week I have been deep in
accounting sh**, if you will forgive the expression.'[245] What he soon
discovered was that Ravan was technically bankrupt, despite Walter
Felgate producing funds of dubious origins. Marilyn describes how 'Mike
didn't know where the money was coming from, and it seemed that Walter
Felgate would go to Mozambique and come back with a suitcase full of
money to pay the printers. . . . Then Mike discovered we were bankrupt. So
he went to Felgate and he said, "I'm here to run this company and it's

---

[244] Coetzee to Tom Rosenthal, 19 March 1983, 1998.8.1, Amazwi.
[245] Kirkwood to Wessel Ebersohn, 23 June 1978, PMA.

bankrupt. I will make public what you've done unless you sell me this company, tomorrow, for R10." And that's what happened.'[246] This led to Kirkwood and Mutloatse becoming directors, in name alone, of what was essentially a bankrupt company.

For both, Ravan's mission could not be separated from its business model. As with other activist publishers, the collective structure was intended to be both a symbol and an active performance of participatory democracy. All staff were intended to participate in decision-making and roles were shared. Advisory committees were established, and a trust was established to oversee the Press and coordinate donor funding beginning in 1984. The trustees included well-respected authors, many of whom had been published by Ravan, including Achmat Dangor, Peter Delius, Ahmed Essop, Nadine Gordimer, Chabani Manganyi, Njabulo Ndebele and Eddie Webster. Peter Randall was also included after his unbanning, along with Beyers Naude and Archbishop Desmond Tutu. Kirkwood described the 'new democratic Ravan' as making great strides in 1984.[247] But in truth the collective was not a success. As McGillian notes, 'Initially these decentralized working environments must have held a certain appeal, but most people who toiled within them eventually discovered they could also be burdensome, inefficient, and alienating.'[248] Tony Morphet suggests that the editorial collective led to 'a steady rise in backstabbing and a steep fall in output':[249]

> Ravan's limited financial resources inevitably placed a heavy burden on their staff. Kirkwood found himself emotionally, intellectually and physically exhausted by the demands of being publisher, editor, commissioning editor, rights negotiator, office manager, fund-raiser, amateur lawyer, police negotiator, public figure, intellectual and proofreader. This led him to restructure Ravan along supposedly 'democratic' and 'participatory' lines, dispensing with all hierarchy and instituting a staff collective as the day-to-day governing body. While this

---

[246] Honikman, interview. [247] Kirkwood to Brian Willan, 29 March 1984, PMA.
[248] McMillian, *Smoking Typewriters*, 10–11. [249] Morphet, 'Child of a special time'.

was in line with the general egalitarian thinking of the anti-
apartheid movement at that time, it led to the progressive
collapse of Ravan's internal structure, administration and
staff morale.[250]

One of the areas that initially flourished but later suffered under collective
management was relationships with authors. Authors regularly dropped in at
the offices, although, as Vladislavic recalls, 'all this talking and advising was
bad business: a commercial publishing house is not meant to be a writing
school.'[251] Kirkwood also went to great lengths to support authors, sometimes
financially, as when he sent an advance that Ravan could ill afford to Noni
Jabavu in Harare. While they enjoyed friendly and informal ties with the
Press, authors were also concerned about the finer details of distribution,
marketing and sales. Throughout the 1980s, the files are full of examples of
authors complaining of a lack of response to their queries. 'I suspect that you
are so busy,' one wrote, diplomatically, 'you don't have time for letters.'[252]
After falling out with Kirkwood, Jabavu was less tactful: 'Tardy communication, non-reply to specific questions, was Mike Kirkwood's treatment of me
(and of other authors, I later discovered).'[253] Authors complained of general
inefficiency, which was 'apparently justified because Ravan is "democratically
run"'.[254] More importantly, there were problems with keeping records and
with paying royalties regularly. This letter is typical of authors' concerns:

> The amount due may not seem like a very large sum, but it is
> a great deal to me. It is my only payment for the five years of
> full-time work which the book took to research and write.
> I know that Ravan Press is not a normal profit-making com-
> pany, but I am trying to make a living out of writing. . . . It has
> been my experience with Ravan Press that it takes several

---

[250] Moss, 'Life and changing times'.   [251] Vladislavic, 'Staffrider'.
[252] Robert Molteno to Kirkwood, 15 June 1983, PMA.
[253] Noni Jabavu to Dorothy Wheeler, 1 June 1983, PMA.
[254] Friedman to Wheeler, 17 August 1986, PMA.

letters over a period of many months before I can usually get
a brief response.[255]

In addition, cash flow was poorly managed, which had a knock-on effect on
production. Authors complained of the erratic publishing schedule or of
being pushed to write quickly and then experiencing long delays in publishing. Kirkwood admitted:

> As you have guessed, we have had a cash flow problem –
> though fortunately in the literal sense rather than in the
> sense of a euphemism for bankruptcy. There's been
> a downturn in the market this year and a lot of our cash is
> locked up in books which aren't selling as quickly as we'd
> like. It's been difficult to keep to our production schedule.[256]

He was also candid about their inefficiency: 'Our accounts side has been in
such a mess that I had to use the last two weeks exclusively to try and get
things right.'[257] After Jessie Duarte was appointed as a bookkeeper in 1984,
matters improved temporarily. Much of her role was placating authors:
'Thank you very much for your patience with our delay in remitting your
royalties to you. Ravan has undergone a very difficult year and through it
we have made some very progressive changes which will improve the
efficiency of our publishing house.'[258] By 1987, Ravan had developed
a financial administration section, in an effort to improve payments and
communication.

However, while *Staffrider* usually ran at a loss, Ravan's books were quite
profitable. Financial statements show a respectable gross profit margin of
33.7 per cent in 1984, on sales of more than R300 000, and 27.9 per cent in
1985, on sales of nearly R500 000. But costs rose at the same time, with a large
staff component leading to a considerable spike in salaries, nearly trebling

---

[255] Kevin Shillington to Ravan, 12 August 1987, PMA.
[256] Kirkwood to Jeff Peires, 27 July 1983, PMA.
[257] Kirkwood to Jeff Peires, 1 May 1981, PMA.
[258] Jessie Duarte to Wessel Ebersohn, November 1984, PMA.

from 1984 to 1985. Thus, although at first Ravan aimed at cost recovery, it later accepted subventions and became increasingly dependent on external funding. Figures for 1987, for example, show foreign grants amounting to around a third of total income; by 1988, the publishing list was deemed unviable without grants. These came largely from donors who were also involved in supporting internal resistance against apartheid in other spheres, including church organisations, Scandinavian aid agencies and the Ford Foundation. Unfortunately, Ravan's generally inefficient record-keeping tested the patience of even very trusting and flexible funders.

Apart from administrative inefficiency, the collective had other consequences. The structure may have been intended to discourage elitism, but it still retained a basic pecking order. For instance, while the male directors' names are highlighted, a variety of less visible men and women worked in the background, often on mundane or laborious tasks. There has also been criticism, especially of *Staffrider*, for its focus on male authors.[259] Moreover, while the staff were racially mixed, the black staff tended to be concentrated around *Staffrider* or in service positions. An example of racial tensions emerged during the publications of James Matthews' *The Park and Other Stories*. He complained about the way in which Chris van Wyk treated him: 'i still declare that chris' actions will alienate black writers and it's not the amount of money he's paid but the attitude he adopts. i still believe fervently in the good work ravan press is doing.'[260] Such interpersonal conflicts arose regularly, with so many passionate personalities gathered in a small and pressurised space. Kirkwood, in particular, could be abrasive as well as charming. Over time, these racial and ideological divisions led to a much more fundamental split.

The Skotaville Split

While many thought of writing as universal and able to transcend the colour line, in practice, segregation was a more powerful force. The attempt to integrate writers' groups into a more multiracial form was thus not long lived.

---

[259] Mofokeng, 'Where are the women?' 41–3; Gqola, 'In search of female staffriders'. Gqola has written further on the role of women in the BCM.

[260] Matthews to Kirkwood, 8 November 1984, PMA. (punctuation in original)

There was a growing feeling that black people should control the production and publishing, as well as the writing, and reject the 'white exploitative editor' and 'the white <u>gurus</u> who control publication out there'.[261] It was also believed that white writers looked down on those authors who valued relevance and social activism over literary standards. As Ravan was perceived as a predominantly white publishing house, even if a radical one, discussions began around the possibility of a separate imprint, Staffrider Press, which would represent the 'black writing' side and be wholly black run.[262] But to many, this did not go far enough. With the influence of Black Consciousness and the ideology of taking back control, authors argued that the problem remained, as Mzamane expressed it, that 'Ravan is in your hands and not in mine or Mothobi's'. Mutloatse thought he was a director in name only and was not included in day-to-day operations, saying, 'I don't regret having been involved with Ravan but there comes a time when you want to do your own thing, be the captain of the ship.'[263] Similarly, Seroke describes feeling alienated: 'The real situation was that the establishment was white owned and decision-making at Ravan had been made into such an amorphous exercise that ordinary workers within Ravan, even us, who were supposedly in charge of *Staffrider* magazine and a series of books, did not know how it came about that these books were published.'[264]

The polarisation within Ravan is intimately related to the cleft that emerged in PEN. The Johannesburg PEN branch disbanded early in 1981, as a result of black writers breaking ranks with their white counterparts. While the writers' aims remained broadly the same, they differed as to the means and ownership of the publishing process.[265] Most black writers believed this was a time for self-sufficiency, although some, like Mafika Gwala, opposed the disbandment. Nadine Gordimer attempted to placate both sides, arguing that 'the move should not be interpreted as reflecting a desire on the part of the black members to dissociate from whites.' Rather, this was the 'wrong historical moment for non-racial

---

[261] M.V. Mzamane to Kirkwood, 6 May 1980, PMA.

[262] Kirkwood to Mzamane, 24 May 1982, PMA

[263] Schwartz, 'Books putting black views'. [264] Seroke, 'Voice of the Voiceless'.

[265] Ndebele, 'The Writers' Movement'; Matshoba, 'Disbandment of PEN'.

collaboration'.[266] The morning after the vote to disband, newspapers announced the formation of the African Writers' Association (AWA), a new body for black writers. At the urging of Es'kia Mphahlele, the members of AWA soon advocated the establishment of their own publishing house. Jaki Seroke recalls, 'In the room, I was the only one who understood the inner workings of a publishing house, so they said, When you have the time, start that publishing house.'[267] And so Seroke and Mutloatse established Skotaville Publishers. The mission was 'to produce black literature that is relevant and contemporary – and to do it under black control from start to finish'.[268] Skotaville was run, at least initially, as a non-profit cooperative, with a board made up mostly of black writers. It was not sustainable, however, without donor funding and experienced familiar problems with banning and harassment.

The split came as a great shock to those associated with Ravan Press. Rose Zwi expressed the emotions felt by white writers and publishers who had been part of PEN: 'Not a hint of this was given to people with whom you had worked so closely for years. It came as a complete shock.'[269] For Kirkwood, the personal sense of betrayal was even more intense. He objected fiercely to being seen as a gatekeeper, but Ravan was placed in a very ambiguous position through this split – as a champion of black writers, yet still a white publisher, with all the baggage that entailed. Andy Mason recalls: 'That was immensely devastating to Mike. It was difficult for him to take on board what was essentially a criticism of his paternalistic role.'[270] Seroke remembers Kirkwood saying he saw the move as a kick in the teeth but insists he was supportive in spite of this, understanding that the underlying intention was to promote black writers and publishers.[271] The split thus did not lead to a complete breaking off of ties. Seroke and Mutloatse still worked with Ravan on some projects and shared similar ideological aims. However, on letterheads from 1982 on, Mutloatse's name is crossed out and Peter Randall's written in.

---

[266] Gordimer, quoted in *Sash*, 25 (4), February 1983, 16.   [267] Seroke, interview.
[268] Van Slambrouck, 'Black South African writers'.   [269] Zwi, 'In conversation'.
[270] Andy Mason, interview with author, February 2017.   [271] Seroke, interview.

Relations with the State

The split with Skotaville is emblematic of larger divisions within South African society. The 1980s saw a series of states of emergency, as the government ramped up its 'total onslaught' to counter the threat of the black majority. Publishers were scrutinised and freedom of information curtailed. Ravan was subject to more state interventions than any other publisher, to the extent that it maintained 'a dubious survival in the borders of the State's favour'.[272] Correspondence was opened and tampered with, phones were bugged, and staff such as Jaki Seroke were detained. The offices were searched and books confiscated. Still more dangerously, authors such as Dikobe were sent letter bombs.

The censorship regime made possible under the 1963 and 1974 acts was harsh:

> Censorship, as far as we are concerned, is one of the many institutional weapons that an oppressive state has at its disposal. Its utilization, whether through the Prisons Act or any other mechanism, is a political act, an act of violence against the culture of resistance in South Africa. By and large, we have sought to challenge that system by trying to push out the frontiers of censorship.[273]

Ravan titles were repeatedly banned, with the Staffrider Series of black authors being particularly hard hit: no fewer than eight of the first thirteen volumes were banned. Matshoba's *Call Me Not a Man* was banned as soon as the second printing came off the presses. Asked how he felt, Matshoba responded: 'At first I thought it should be treated with the kind of contempt it deserved. Later on, I began to feel sort of depressed by it. I found myself almost censoring my work, censoring what I was writing. But I think now, after two weeks, I'm getting over it.'[274] Kirkwood noted that this banning 'created a storm of anger in the black community. . . .

---

[272] Kirkwood to Faber & Faber, 25 October 1979, PMA.

[273] Kirkwood, 'Informal discussion', 30.

[274] Quoted in Powell, 'Writing is part of the struggle', 10.

Staffrider series flyer (Source: Amazwi)

The banning is thus interpreted as an attack by the State on the black community as a whole.'[275]

Most writers refused to appeal against a banning, on principle, and Ravan supported them in this stand.[276] Gillian Booth-Yudelman suggests

---

[275] Kirkwood, 'Banning of Book'.   [276] Mtshali, 'Pressing for change'.

that this stance may be viewed in two ways: appealing was undesirable because it suggested an acceptance of apartheid policy, but the lack of appeals may also have induced a certain level of self-censorship, which may ironically have been more effective than direct intervention.[277] Ravan was not inclined to self-censor, as a review of Achmat Dangor's poetry collection, *Bulldozer*, acknowledges: 'This [Staffrider] series provides vivid evidence of the disastrous political situation, and it remains remarkable that such verse is permitted under the government's repressive censorship. Either the bold can achieve more than is usually admitted, or censors assume poetry is not a genre that will inflame the masses.'[278] To avoid the attention of the Security Police, some manuscripts were edited and laid out off premises. Julie Frederikse has described working on *None but Ourselves* with Andy Mason at her house in 1982: 'We listened to Bob Marley and hung a sign over his light table with a quote from Redemption Song: "We got to fulfill da book."'[279]

The case of *The Third Day of September* clearly illustrates Ravan's relations with the state. The author, Isaac Rantete, wrote to Ravan in September 1984: 'I would like the notes which I wrote in reference with the recent unrests of the Vaal to be published as a book. What I wrote is true and is accompanied by photos which I shot to confirm the statement.'[280] Ravan received many such letters – handwritten, on paper torn from notebooks and schoolbooks – but this one struck an immediate chord. Seeing an opportunity for a new series based on witness testimony, dubbed the Storyteller Series, Kirkwood edited and published Rantete's title extremely quickly, within a month. There are conflicting stories around the illustrations: production notes suggest that the quality of the photographs was poor, so artist Goodman Mabote was asked to produce adaptations. Later, this adaptation is framed as a means of obscuring the identities of those involved from the security police. The original photographs were either destroyed by Kirkwood or lost in the post.

The Third Day of September was published in October 1984 and widely reviewed. Most reviews lauded the achievement of writing history 'as it

---

[277] Quoted in Booth-Yudelman, 'South African political prison-literature'.

[278] Povey, Review.   [279] Frederikse, 'Author's reflections'.

[280] Rantete to Ravan Press, 14 September 1984, PMA.

happened': 'Ravan Press continues courageously to publish works that provide outlets for new South African voices. This is the first in its Storyteller Series, which "welcomes books on all subjects – current events, life stories, humour, things that happened yesterday or long ago."'[281] The state found there was too much emphasis on violence and confiscated copies of the book in Sebokeng – even though they did not know whether or not it had been banned. Rantete was then detained under the Internal Security Act, and the book banned. Kirkwood had foreseen this possibility, writing to Anne Walmsley at *Index on Censorship*, 'in the hope that if something happens – banning, harassment, etc. – you will be in a position to react quickly and accurately.'[282] Much of the account later given in *Index on Censorship* is copied verbatim from these letters and a press release written after Rantete's detention. Ravan appealed to the Publications Board, successfully: 'Distribution of the book resumed. It went well in the city bookshops because of media attention. But distribution continued to be difficult in Sebokeng itself: the police had succeeded in intimidating both distributors and readership.'[283] In fact, Ravan found after this experience that informal distributors had to be provided with a special 'letter of authorisation . . . if anything goes wrong'.[284]

The application of censorship was far from consistent or even logical, as scholars such as Peter McDonald have shown. For instance, David Martin and Phyllis Johnson's *Struggle for Zimbabwe* went unnoticed in hardcover under the Faber & Faber imprint, but when Ravan produced a paperback edition in 1982, customs officials embargoed it. Faber was frustrated: 'It's surely crazy for a ban to be slapped on a book which, in its hardback form, was found to be acceptable and was very prominently serialized throughout the South African press.'[285] When Kirkwood found that the Ravan paperback edition had in fact been declared 'not undesirable', he complained, 'Enlightened changes in policy are being handed down by the PAB, but the people responsible for implementing the laws are ill-informed. . . .

---

[281] Segal, Review.   [282] Kirkwood to Anne Walmsley, 17 October 1984, PMA.

[283] Index on Censorship, 'Johannes Rantete'.

[284] 'Censorship and harassment: Advice for Ravan agents', undated letter, PMA.

[285] Mike McLennan to Kirkwood, 5 July 1982, PMA.

Publishers, booksellers and the public are suffering because of this confusion.'[286] The changes in censorship policy were slowly but erratically applied during the 1980s, and publishers such as David Philip made a particular point of appealing for the unbanning of certain titles so that new editions could be produced in its Africasouth series. Ravan saw books such as Matshoba's *Call Me Not a Man* and Madingoane's *Afrika my Beginning*, both banned in 1979, being unbanned by 1985. Such titles could then be read in South Africa for the first time.

Even as censorship eased, state intervention intensified. In July 1985, the government declared a state of emergency. The new powers gave the police the authority to confiscate books for being 'subversive', and to lay charges against authors, publishers, printers and booksellers: 'in one way or another, "emergency" has existed in this country for decades, but now harassment, detention, torture and death exist in the context of an enforced public silence.'[287] Ravan continued to disregard threats, publishing obviously provocative titles such as Suttner and Cronin's book celebrating the anniversary of the Freedom Charter in 1986. The book, aiming to 'provide a resource for activists rather than to serve as a definitive text for academics and students',[288] was predictably banned for not being 'an objective historical account . . . but an attempt to promote the revolutionary ideals of the ANC'.[289] The censors also objected to the accessibility of the book, as this increased the size of the potential audience, especially among young black people. Advocate Gilbert Marcus was again asked to appeal the banning and also to give an opinion on titles such as *A Different Kind of War*, *The Struggle and the Future*, *Two Dogs and Freedom* and *The Right to Learn*: 'We would like you to comment on how the books we have submitted could "offend" the state, which laws they contravene if this is at all possible, we realise that the new emergency measures are very wide and almost anything could be determined "undesire-able" [sic].'[290] Part of the appeal included an argument against the censorship

---

[286] 'Censorship: 'Confusion over the rules', *Financial Mail*, 3 March 1982.

[287] Driver, '"Appendix II" South Africa', 170.

[288] Connor, 'Remembering the Freedom Charter', 112.

[289] Directorate of Publications, P 86/06/43, PMA.

[290] Jessie Duarte to Gilbert Marcus, c. 1986, PMA.

committees, which had widespread powers, lacked representivity, were not politically accountable, paid special attention to political publications and regularly flouted their own guidelines.[291]

When the state of emergency was renewed in 1986, Kirkwood joined the Anti-Censorship Action Committee (ACAC). The ACAC argued that censorship was achieved less by formal means than by intimidation via the emergency laws. When Mark Orkin published a book on disinvestment, he used the platform generated by interest in the book to support this stance:

> I took the complaint you made at the first censorship meet-
> ing about diffident writers very seriously, and in my bit at
> the *Fair Lady* book week explicitly dwelt on the courage of
> my publisher in pressing ahead with a difficult book at
> a difficult time, keeping the flame of scientific truth alight
> against the draught of the monopoly-owned English-
> language press ideology, etc.

He added, only half jokingly, 'only there was no evident Ravan represen-tative to relay the praise.'[292]

The harassment reached new levels in 1987. First, typesetter Esther Maleka was detained under the emergency regulations. She had previously been arrested for recruiting for the ANC and was active in the Federation of South African Women (FEDCRAW) and the United Democratic Front (UDF). Then, in October 1987, Ravan's offices were firebombed. The *Star* newspaper reported that around R15 000 worth of books were damaged, and many records destroyed.[293] A press release noted, 'This is the fifth time that persons have attempted to enter or succeeded in gaining entry to the premises of Ravan Press with the intention to do harm.'[294] Police raids became

---

[291] U. Manoim to the Publications Appeal Board, 14 July 1986, PMA.

[292] Mike Orkin to Jessie Duarte, 29 December 1986, PMA.

[293] 'Three armed men fire-bomb offices of liberal press', *Star*, 19 March 1987. Later staffers would use this incident repeatedly as an excuse for missing records.

[294] 'Incident of Friday, 30 October 1987', Press release, 1987, PMA.

a regular occurrence, although the government's policy of 'repressive tolerance', meant it wished 'to establish an image of openness and tolerance while
maintaining a high degree of control over outspoken opposition media'.[295]

Exit Kirkwood

Amid this onslaught, Mike Kirkwood left Ravan, and the fiction that it could
sustain itself as a collective collapsed. Kirkwood's reasons for leaving were
a complex mix of the personal, professional and political. Marilyn recalls that
he first suggested emigrating after his disillusionment with the falling-out with
Skotaville and the disbandment of PEN. At around the same time, however,
he also became involved with a younger woman. Andy Mason comments,
'Mike was a very glamorous guy, he was good looking, a very intense
personality. And he got involved in a very embarrassing sexual liaison with
the woman who would become his next wife. . . . It caused a huge fracas, and
a big bust-up.'[296] After the divorce, Marilyn left Ravan, which left a gaping
hole in distribution and administration. Another factor was Mike's deteriorat-
ing relationship with Peter Randall. Several sources suggest that Randall took
the opportunity of the turmoil in Mike's personal life to quietly force him out.
Marilyn says bluntly that Kirkwood was fired for perceived (but not actual)
financial irregularities. She describes a tense personal relationship between the
two and attributes this in part to the recognition Kirkwood received:

> Ravan Press, before our time, had been this publishing
> house that would print 1 500 copies of a book and sell 500.
> So, amongst a few cognoscenti and political people it was
> well known. But not further. But it was a household name by
> the time I left, and so was Mike. Because that was my job,
> and I made him a household name. And I think Peter
> Randall got very bitter about that.[297]

Another reason mentioned was the political situation, which sent many
writers and publishers into exile: 'Mike was one of the chief editors, and

---

[295] Driver, 'Appendix: South Africa', 168.   [296] Mason, interview.
[297] Honikman, interview.

had been the firm's director since 1977. Since the State of Emergency was reimposed following my visit, he has left the country, moving to England.'[298]

Amid all of these factors, Kirkwood relocated to London in 1987. This led to an immediate drop in production and a lack of management. Ravan was in debt to its printers and surviving on piecemeal funding from grants. It continued to be supported by trustees such as Ndebele, Matshoba and Serote. The remaining staff did their best to explain the situation to authors and keep the press afloat, as letters show:

> Mike has recently relocated to London, and will be editing for Ravan from there for the next couple of years.[299]
>
> You may have heard that Ravan is going through a difficult patch. We have been experiencing some very serious financial problems, but it looks as if we'll survive.[300]

Andries Oliphant joined the staff to work on *Staffrider* and describes the Press in a state of disarray: 'everyone was responsible and no one accountable.'[301] For an interim period, the trust brought in two commercial publishers, Jonathan Ball and Philip Neville, to implement emergency measures to prevent a complete collapse. They sought to drastically reduce staff and overheads, curtail publishing expenditure, negotiate with creditors and bring in additional funding.[302] They also had to negotiate the rather tangled matter of who owned shares in Ravan and try to fend off a legal challenge from George Shuttleworth that related to Felgate's shareholding in Ravan.[303] A particular issue about ownership arose with Mike's exit: who held shares in Ravan, and were they actually worth anything? Kirkwood relinquished his shares to the Ravan Trust, but Marilyn had successfully

[298]   Brummer, *Processed World*.
[299]   Ivan Vladislavic to Yvonne Burgess, 11 May 1987, PMA.
[300]   Vladislavic to Bob Edgar, 4 December 1987, PMA.
[301]   Andries Oliphant, interview with author, 12 September 2019.
[302]   'Ravan Press (Pty) Ltd: Report of the Management Advisors', undated report (c. 1988), PMA.
[303]   Notes from editorial meetings, undated, PMA.

negotiated for a proportion of the shares to be transferred to her as part of the divorce settlement. These were eventually returned to the trust, after negotiations and the payment of a nominal 'dividend'.[304]

Ball and Neville were successful in staving off the creditors, but their proposals for drastic restructuring and an emphasis on profit were badly received. Dorothy Wheeler wrote to an author, 'Our Management Adviser turned out to be a bit of a disillusionment and a number of the trustees had to become very actively involved to see us through until a manager could be installed.'[305] A complete implosion was prevented, but this was a turning point for Ravan.

5 Transition

The liberation movements were unbanned in 1990, and Nelson Mandela released from prison. With the first inclusive elections of April 1994 and the installation of the African National Congress–led government, the era of state censorship ended and freedom of expression was enshrined in the Constitution. The cultural boycott came to an end, and South African businesses – including publishers – were welcomed back into the international community. Ravan celebrated twenty-one years in 1993, sending out an advertisement that read:

> For twenty-one years, Ravan has been at the cutting edge of indigenous South African publishing of quality. While the social context within which Ravan publishes has changed – and, indeed, continues to change – the original guiding principles of excellence in critical, progressive and independent publishing remain unaltered.
>
> Whether in the field of creative writing or social engagement, progressive education or working-class history, Ravan has kept alive a flame of freedom and democracy which at times flickered dangerously low in other areas of society.

[304] Jonathan Ball to Kirkwood, 14 March 1988, PMA.
[305] Wheeler to Jeff Guy, 27 July 1988, PMA.

> As Ravan celebrates twenty-one years of publishing, its
> staff and trustees salute all those who have kept, and continue
> to keep, a critical and independent spirit of publishing alive.

Within a few years, this critical spirit had ceased to exist.

Ravan did not survive the South African transition, due to both internal failings and a hostile external environment. As an anti-apartheid publisher, Ravan's decline after the end of apartheid now seems inevitable. However, a fierce battle was waged to reposition it. All expectations were that the oppositional publishers would have a head start in publishing under the new dispensation, due to their reputation, backlist and connections – and especially Ravan, with its radical outlook and support for Black Consciousness. It has been argued that 'Ravan was uniquely placed to continue the democratization process that so enlivened South African literature and historiography after 1976.'[306] Instead, 'Almost overnight, some of the symbols, issues and modes of operation which had influenced nearly two decades of Ravan's publishing became inappropriate. The new threat was anachronism.'[307]

Reorganisation

Even before the end of apartheid, the Press was in disarray. In late 1988, Glenn Moss accepted the position of director at the ailing Press. He soon found, to his dismay, that closure could be more viable than reorganisation:

> [Ravan's] weaknesses as a publishing *company* were the
> direct result of its strengths as a socially-engaged and
> committed *publisher*, and its internal systems in all the
> basics of publishing – warehousing, marketing, financial
> management, planning, sales representation – were so
> flawed as to defy restructuring.[308]

Moss, a former student activist, had worked in the non-profit sector in South Africa for years and was well known for his work on *Work in*

---

[306] Lewis, Review. [307] Moss, 'Life and Changing Times'.
[308] Moss, 'Ringing the Changes', 14, emphasis in original.

Progress. 'I thought,' Moss wrote, 'that after 18 years in "alternative" organisations I had seen just about everything possible in areas of inefficiency, irresponsibility, incompetence and general left *slap*ness: but Ravan has shown me a new low in all those areas.'[309] The administration was in chaos, books were not coming out or being marketed, and few systems were being followed. Attention had to focus on administration and funding, and Moss lamented that 'the energy and time which had to be put into remaking the publishing house detracted from the publishing programme.'[310] He also recognised that 'a mountain of problems and issues remain to be resolved before Ravan can retake its rightful place as South Africa's leading oppositional publishing house.'[311]

One of these issues was the unaffordable staff complement. Immediate restructuring led to retrenchments, and the retention of a smaller staff; Monica Seeber was appointed assistant to the manager and Gary Hirst, financial manager. Editorial functions were outsourced while one production manager was retained (Jeff Lok), and a core group was kept on for warehousing and sales and promotions. Over time, Moss brought in former colleague Ingrid Obery for editorial and desktop publishing. Inevitably, the restructuring led to resentment from former staff, as well as placing a heavy burden on the smaller team. Restructuring also led to the loss of *Staffrider* to the Congress of South African Writers (COSAW): Andries Oliphant was managing *Staffrider*; however, as things became more precarious he started COSAW Publishing, and the magazine was transferred. Although *Staffrider* had been a fairly regular quarterly at first, output had slowed from about 1983; the sequential volume numbering obscures the decline to only one issue a year in the mid-1980s. This was not due to a drop in submissions but rather funding and editorial selection. Seeber remembers sorting the correspondence: 'When I had a big pile I would go to Andries's office, next to mine. I remember standing in the doorway and throwing all of these at him. He would say, I'm drowning in bad poetry!'[312]

---

[309] Moss to Jeff Peires, 26 October 1988, PMA. *Slap* is Afrikaans, meaning sloppy.
[310] Moss to authors, 13 July 1990, PMA.
[311] Moss to Colin Smuts, 25 January 1989, PMA.
[312] Monica Seeber, interview with author, 16 September 2019.

Another effect of the inefficient administration was poor relations with authors. The editorial files contain letter after letter apologising for their past treatment and assuring them that Ravan would be rebuilding. Even authors of the status of Nadine Gordimer had received no answers to their letters or queries: 'I was dismayed,' she wrote, 'over the inefficiency followed by the discourtesy I have experienced at Ravan over the past two years. I am sure that now you have taken over the reins the publishing house will regain its special place in our cultural life.'[313] Moss sympathised with another author: 'Reviewing the history of this publication, I can see that your relationship with Ravan has had its ups and downs, and you most certainly suffered the frustrations of Ravan's "difficult years."'[314] Vladislavic and Seeber reorganised the filing, so that contracts and correspondence would be more systematic. The many disgruntled authors appreciated the more businesslike approach and welcomed 'the first sign of efficiency received from Ravan'.[315]

As ever, quality and economic viability had to be balanced; to put it bluntly, Ravan needed money. The ability to publish without regard for profit had rested on external funding, which all but dried up: 'This withdrawal of funding fell heavily on non-government organizations, including the independent presses, which had played an important role in popular literacy projects, but now, unsubsidized, were forced to close as multinational publishers increasingly took over the South African book market.'[316] With the help of the trustees, Moss was able to attract some funding; added to this, he mandated 'the cutting of overheads wherever possible, extreme caution in acceptance of new manuscripts, and a gradual move into new areas of publishing'.[317] In practice, it was not easy to balance efficient business principles with a commitment to social justice, as increasing risk aversion shifted Ravan away from its original ethos. For a time, though, the strategy worked: the *Financial Mail* commented on Ravan's

---

[313] Gordimer to Moss, 12 November 1988, PMA.

[314] Moss to Louise Kretzschmar, 18 June 1990, PMA.

[315] Jeff Opland to Moss, 12 August 1991, PMA. [316] Trimbur, 'Popular Literacy'.

[317] Moss, 'Report and assessment of the activities of Ravan Press for the period January-December 1992', February 1993, PMA.

'remarkable turn-around'.[318] Peter Randall, now chairman of the trust, was cautiously optimistic: 'Ravan is in a significantly healthier position, financially and in terms of management, than it was.'[319] During this period, Randall continued to play an important role, albeit in the background. He vetted manuscripts and made editorial decisions; he also served as acting manager when Moss was away.

Ravan's reputation rested not on its financial viability but on its publishing: 'Books from the cutting edge of South African publishing'. The pathbreaking literature that had become a feature of Ravan's list declined in favour of contemporary social and political books. This was not so much a conscious change in editorial policy as a combined effect of a greater focus on non-fiction, poor sales and rather indifferent submissions.[320] Books that would sell fewer than 1 000 to 2 000 copies within a year were rejected. Moss apologised to one author: 'When Ravan still received donor funds for exploratory publishing with a limited market we could undertake such projects. Now that we are reliant on our sales and income, we have to be confident that the potential market is of sufficient magnitude to warrant publication.'[321] The literary list came to rely on unsolicited manuscripts and returning authors and was often unprofitable. Ivan Vladislavic, who continued to act as a freelance editor, noted in this regard: 'We have not published many plays partly because it is very difficult to sell plays. The tapering of interest in the theatre has made us carefully vet the publication of plays.'[322] One of the few drama titles from this period is an expanded edition of Zakes Mda's plays.

The focus of the list in the early 1990s was politics, usually linked to labour and indirectly to the ANC. Moss admits that his own interests lay in these areas: 'the contemporary politics list and the academic list is what just came to us, because that's where I came from.'[323] 'I don't know,' he adds, 'if the publishing was nearly as exciting as it had been, or as innovative, but the

---

[318] 'Ravan takes off,' *Financial Mail*, 24 March 1989: 62–4.

[319] Randall to Frank England, 24 November 1988, PMA.

[320] Moss, 'Life and Times of Ravan'. [321] Moss to [author], 10 March 1994, PMA.

[322] Khan, 'Who reads what's written'.

[323] Glenn Moss, interview with author, 30 May 2016.

world was also changing.' Many titles focused on the anticipated transition – *Beyond Apartheid*, as one book was called. These titles are oriented towards the future and were valuable in the midst of a media blackout: one reviewer found, 'The recent clampdown on information makes Mark Orkin's *Disinvestment, the Struggle and the Future* especially welcome. Subtitled "What Black South Africans Really Think", it provides a view the media have tried hard to hide.'[324] Similarly, Shelagh Gastrow's *Who's Who* was popular as a reference with libraries, although the market was soon saturated with similar titles from other publishers.[325] The activist mission of these publications continued: 'this new *South African Review* ... is often provocative and does not pretend to be "neutral". It is a very good example of what is sometimes called "committed scholarship", the kind that believes that truth must imply a moral judgment.'[326]

The current affairs titles were important for the time, but it is not for them that Ravan reached the top of the league in the Noma Award.[327] These awards were given for groundbreaking historical analysis and important literary works, such as Njabulo Ndebele's *Bonolo and the Peach Tree*, which won in 1993. Its publication history exposes both the successes and fault lines at Ravan. The title, aimed at children, was produced in two editions, for schools and trade, and went through multiple reprints. It also sold into US schools through a deal with Harcourt Brace. However, the author was unhappy with the production process. In fact, he was so displeased that he withdrew a manuscript of literary essays, already accepted for publication as early as 1988. The problems arose because of internal disputes: the title was positioned as a co-publication between Ravan and Fountain Press, the children's imprint developed by Isobel Randall and Gerald de Villiers of Hodder. The lines of responsibility were unclear and misunderstandings arose, leading to production delays and disputes, all aired in front of the author. Isobel's often turbulent relationship with other Ravan employees came into sharp focus on this project; one of her own letters reveals that she was tempted to

---

[324] Connor, 'Remembering the Freedom Charter', 156.

[325] Moss to Steven Friedman, 29 September 1993, PMA.

[326] Egan, 'Perspectives of the future'.   [327] Mitchell, 'Top of the list', 2.

'interfere' out of a sense of 'duty' to the authors.[328] Both Obery and Moss accused her of being unprofessional and disruptive.[329]

Significant historical studies continued to be submitted, and to break new ground. In 1992, Tim Couzens' biography *Tramp Royal* won the *Sunday Times* Alan Paton Award; Nadine Gordimer called it a 'lovely, unclassifiable book'.[330] Other titles included Jeff Peires' definitive historical study *The Dead Will Arise: Nongqawuse and the Great Xhosa Cattle-Killing Movement of 1856–7*, with co-publication in the United States and the United Kingdom;[331] Julie Frederikse's *Unbreakable Thread* included interviews with anti-apartheid activists, linked by a theory of non-racialism; and Daniel Kunene's biography of Thomas Mofolo remains the classic work on this writer. There was also, strangely for this list, a book on the popular band Mango Groove. For novels, such as Frank Anthony's *The Journey*, Moss sought subventions: 'In strictly commercial terms, it is a wholly unviable publishing project, but Ravan's commitment to uncovering and developing new literature – especially by black South African authors – makes it a worthy project.'[332] Other significant works included Paul Hotz's novel *Muzukuru*, based on interviews with Zimbabwean freedom fighters; Ahmed Essop's *Noorjehan and Other Stories*; and Hein Grosskopf's *Artistic Graves*, the only thriller ever published by Ravan. The latter title received extensive media coverage due to the author's political background, but CNA still declined to order copies.

In 1994, Ravan worked with the Centre for Policy Studies to put together a book about the elections. Steven Friedman objected to the idea of a 'quick and dirty instant book', but Moss knew that the election would stir up interest and create a ready market. He thus suggested that rather than compromising quality, the publishing process could be speeded up:

> Where we are working with competent authors who are
> able to write well, and where we can receive a manuscript

---

[328] Isobel Randall to Ravan, 8 July 1991, PMA.

[329] Ingrid Obery to Randall, 10 July 1991; Moss to Randall, 10 July 1991, PMA.

[330] Hofmeyr, Review. [331] Smaldone, Review.

[332] Moss, 'Motivation to utilise funds supplied by the ICCO', 21 May 1991, PMA.

> in a word processing programme, standardised and written
> to agreed specifications, our processes allow for remark-
> ably fast production of final pages. To some extent, this is
> because some of our staff involved in editing and produc-
> tion came from a magazine tradition, rather than the slower
> world of book production; given the right project, they are
> more than willing to reactivate deadline driven publishing
> (including final editing, proofing and setting). Books nor-
> mally do not justify those procedures, and in addition, the
> quality of final manuscripts we receive often forces Ravan
> into very time-consuming and extensive editing and
> rewriting.[333]

After a blunder-ridden publishing process, Friedman refused to work with
Ravan again. But this quote also reveals that Ravan could no longer afford
to invest in its authors with its former levels of intensive editing.

Transformation and Survival

The impact of the new government can most clearly be seen in educational
publishing, the largest and most lucrative sector. The transition to an
integrated education system created many opportunities for publishers.
However, there were fears that biased selection policies would continue,
if not countered by 'fair opportunities and transparent processes governing
book selection and provision'.[334] With the restructuring and amalgamation
of the existing departments of education into a single central department,
the ANC needed a textbook provision policy. In 1993–1994, they published
'An Implementation Plan for Education and Training', with guidelines on
textbook publishing and evaluation:

> The extent to which a new government intervenes in shap-
> ing the course of educational publishing therefore depends
> on the extent to which publishers commit themselves visibly

---

[333] Moss to Friedman, 8 November 1993, PMA.
[334] Moss to Friedman, 8 November 1993, PMA

to the development of a local publishing industry which
fosters indigenous thought, democracy and educational
development; and which reflects the composition, needs
and concerns of all of South Africa's people.[335]

John Samuel, head of the ANC Department of Education, also spelled out
the role of the government in formulating a book development policy,
supporting a reading culture, building a relationship with educational
publishers and drawing on the expertise of anti-apartheid publishers.[336]
Moss summarised,

Players in the vital interface between education and publishing need a proven track record, credibility with key policy
groups and a firm indigenous base within South Africa.
Ravan, with over two decades of progressive, critical, independent publishing of quality, meet these criteria. The
enemy is no longer apartheid, but the power of those
transnational and other interests which tend to dominate
educational publishing.[337]

However, hopes were dashed when Samuel's detailed recommendations
were not implemented, and the new government turned to the established
publishers. Moreover, 'Corruption, endemic in the apartheid-era, quickly
became embedded in new processes.'[338] Rumours of private deals were
rife, but, Moss notes, 'Ravan was in many ways the best placed of the
publishers to try and develop special relationships, but we were both
unwilling and unable to maximise it.'[339] Publishers made a deliberate
attempt to reposition themselves to take advantage of the new dispensation: Macmillan's mission became 'Publishing to serve' and Kagiso's

[335] John Samuel, paper delivered at Sached/NECC conference, 1993.
[336] John Samuel, paper delivered at Sached/NECC conference, 1993, 15–19.
[337] Moss, 'Life and Times of Ravan', 146.
[338] Wessels, 'Challenge and the crisis', 96; Chisholm, 'Textbook saga'.
[339] Moss, interview.

'Making education accessible to all South Africans'. A number of black empowerment deals were also negotiated. For instance, in 1993, Thebe Investment Corporation, the ANC's trading arm, entered into an arrangement with the British multinational Macmillan, with a minority interest from Skotaville, to establish Nolwazi Educational Publishers. Maskew Miller Longman sold half its shares to Khula Educational Investments, as Director Mike Peacock defended: 'We feel that for all people to share in the wealth of our nation, more black South Africans need to gain access to ownership and management of business. . . . This is not tokenism.'[340] But these deals *were* seen as tokenism and were controversial. Moss complained,

> Historically discredited players who only a few short years ago talked the language of Christian National Education suddenly present themselves as torch-bearers of liberation, democracy and progressive education. The capital which they accumulated on the back of Bantu Education and privileged relationships with educational departments is now being poured into advertising campaigns proclaiming their commitment to a new social order.[341]

Working within an uncertain system, the newly repositioned publishers did not face an easy transition. From 1996, there was a drastic cutback in textbook expenditure in anticipation of a new curriculum. At the same time, there was disruption in bookselling, as the CNA chain stopped book purchases and later had to liquidate. As a result, many publishers were forced to downsize.[342]

With even the large publishers affected, David Philip warned that 'the futures of most oppositional publishers are at risk unless they can find funding from inside South Africa or become self-supporting.'[343] In the absence of external funding, the only option was to find new revenue streams. Plans thus

---

[340] Efrat, 'New ownership scramble', 8. [341] Moss, 'Educational Publishing', 5.

[342] Kantey, 'Provision of textbooks'; Prabhakaran, 'Crisis hits educational publishers', 1.

[343] Philip, 'Book Publishing', 45.

focused on sustainability: 'the changed circumstances in South Africa have caused Ravan to plan for self-sufficiency within the next two years, and this has imposed a policy of commercial viability on the organisation wherever possible.'[344] In an interview in 1991, Moss saw this as 'a question of survival':

> It is going to have an enormous effect on the books we put out. It could affect the number of titles published – and publishers will have to be a lot more careful about the financial viability of the titles we select. We will also have to take on more books for commercial reasons. In terms of professionalism it is not necessarily a bad thing, but in terms of willingness to take chances and to experiment it is a disaster.[345]

There was very little room for 'error or exploration'.[346] Moreover, other publishers were now also encroaching on Ravan's core areas:

> Whereas once upon a time only Ravan and one or two other minor players were doing our sorts of books, now there is stiff competition from a host of multi-nationals with South African offices and a range of Jonny-come-latelies who see our traditional areas of publishing as potentially lucrative. All of this raises questions about Ravan's future trajectory.[347]

'I am a little concerned,' Moss added, 'that some of the houses moving into our traditional areas are able to mobilise the greater resources for origination, promotions and repping than at least Ravan can.'[348] Faced with this context, Ravan actively commissioned new work, especially on issues of transformation and business, and tried to build a presence in the schoolbook market; Monica Seeber calls Moss 'obsessed' with the schools market. She bought

---

[344] Moss to John Campbell, 25 February 1991, PMA.
[345] Moss, quoted in Hotz, 'Publishers' problems', 22.
[346] Moss to Stephen Hayward, 31 August 1993, PMA.
[347] Moss to Julie Frederikse, 5 July 1991, PMA.
[348] Moss to David and Marie Philip, 22 March 1990, 2009.92.1.1, Amazwi.

rights to Es'kia Mphahlele's *Down Second Avenue* to publish a Sepedi translation.[349] While this could have been an important new path – local language publishing – the work was never published as it was considered insufficiently profitable. Another way to reach the education market was through co-publishing. One example was Luli Callinicos's history volumes, co-published with Maskew Miller Longman (MML). This was not very successful. Clive Gillitt of MML attributed the low sales to the milieu: 'with the "cooling off" of the political situation, there has been a widely acknowledged falling off of interest in this type of publication. It seems that these publications sold better when the Nationalist Party was being more rigid and dogmatic in its approach to politics.'[350]

It was a time for small publishers to seek common solutions. With David Philip, Moss was instrumental in setting up a new publishers' group – the Independent Publishers' Association of South Africa (IPASA) – in 1989, to advocate against censorship and to press for a more diverse publishing industry. With Skotaville, the publishers also developed a short-lived project on 'Promoting a Reading Culture for Democracy', which would see some of their backlist titles bought for distribution to schools and libraries. Moss and Philip went further, investigating the possibility of exploiting economies of scale through joint projects, while retaining separate identities. In 1993, they developed a proposal 'to establish a new indigenous publishing house to undertake the production of educational textbooks appropriate to a post-apartheid society', to be called Philip and Ravan Educational Publishers (PREP).[351] But eventually it was decided that putting two weaknesses together was not going to create a strength.[352]

Business Rescue?

The trust decided a buyer must be found, and Moss approached Gerald de Villiers at Hodder & Stoughton Educational SA. De Villiers had co-published a number of children's titles with Ravan over the years, so

---

[349] Seeber, interview. [350] Clive Gillitt to Moss, 20 September 1993, PMA.

[351] Richard Rosenthal, 'Proposal concerning the establishment of a public interest education publishing house', 21 April 1993, 2009.92.1.1, Amazwi.

[352] Moss, interview.

there was an existing relationship. He jumped at the opportunity, buying 76 per cent equity in March 1994, with the remaining 24 per cent vested in the Ravan Trust. The deal gave Hodder renewed credibility in the new South Africa, 'in return for access to resources, representation in the rest of Africa and the understanding that Hodder would provide venture capital for specific initiatives'.[353] Oliphant calls this 'the strategy practised by local and multi-national publishers of acquiring or founding imprints with anti-apartheid pedigrees as a means of respositioning themselves in a changed political context'.[354]

In a circular to authors, Moss was at pains to emphasise the positive aspects of the deal: 'Hodder wished to acquire an interest in Ravan Press precisely because it is Ravan, and because of its history, backlist and standing. Hodder has a high opinion of Ravan and its publishing, and has no desire for the core nature of Ravan's current programme, ethos and culture to change.'[355] He went on: 'This wasn't a hostile takeover or a buy out. ... They have guaranteed our editorial independence.' With the infusion of funding, Ravan would be able to produce a wider range of books and expand its marketing. Little changed immediately in terms of staffing or structure, with De Villiers joining the Editorial Committee, but the staff were relocated from Braamfontein to Randburg. While the aim had been to reorient the backlist so that it could be exploited for the schools market, the focus shifted away from educational titles:

> Realising that it would be foolish, given the fierce competition from strongly-resourced publishers, to attempt an expansion into new markets or to experiment with new subject areas in established markets, Ravan intends to exploit to the fullest the niches where its assets are most valued: the intelligent reading public, the tertiary education sector and the business sector in which it has successfully established a foothold in the last four years.[356]

[353] Cloete, 'Alternative Publishing', 50.
[354] Oliphant, 'From Colonialism to Democracy', 121.
[355] Pretorius, 'Local publishers in flux', 38.   [356] Seeber, 'Appeal by Ravan Press'.

At first, the new dispensation seemed to work well. In 1995, Ravan scored a publishing coup with the publication of Joe Slovo's unfinished autobiography. After Slovo's death, Moss had considered commissioning a biography, until Slovo's widow Helena Dolny told him about 'a tatty folder of writing which he had carried around for years'.[357] Moss negotiated for the 'fragments' to form the basis of an autobiography. The Slovo book was launched at a 'rather dazzling affair', co-hosted with CNA.[358] It was well attended, with Nelson Mandela delivering a tribute. The book reached number two on the Exclusive Books bestseller list within a week and was one of Ravan's most successful books ever.

Moreover, an attempt was made to capitalise on the backlist through the Ravan Writers Series, books which 'still have something to say'.[359] Another reissue was *I Write What I Like*, a collection of writings originally published shortly after Steve Biko's death in detention. The reissuing strategy led to Ravan being called a 'shell imprint dedicated to its backlist',[360] but this was unfair, as new titles were also being produced. For instance, former staffer Chris van Wyk's novel *Year of the Tapeworm* was well received in 1996. The reviewer Maureen Isaccson noted a lack of marketing: 'it was not run on the cog of the publicity machine that frequently pushes mediocre books into the forefront of our bookstores. Sadly, as is too often the case with local works, it ran on no cog at all.'[361] This is a strange indictment, given that the Hodder deal was intended to boost working capital and marketing. Other new titles focused on Voices from Robben Island, nation-building, and the interface between labour and business; an introductory reader for health professionals also sold surprisingly well. However, a number of authors who would previously have submitted their work to Ravan began to seek other publishers. The perception was that Ravan's mission had shifted, and there were persistent rumours that the Press was about to close.[362]

---

[357] 'How to be red and read', *Mail & Guardian*, 10–16 November 1995.

[358] Moss to Tim Hely Hutchinson, 1995, PMA.

[359] 'Ravan renews the best of the past', *Mail & Guardian*, 31 March–6 April 1995, 42.

[360] *South African Review of Books*, September/October 1996.

[361] Isaacson, 'Quirky, subversive voice'.　[362] Morphet, 'Child of a special time'.

Moss found it increasingly difficult to work within the confines of 'accounting publishing', which only intensified after Tim Hely-Hutchinson's Headline bought Hodder: 'It made structural adjustment look delicate.'[363] The interest in the bottom line sidelined all other considerations, and Ravan was not considered sufficiently profitable as a subsidiary.[364] As Tony Morphet commented, 'Big capital, long-term planning and strict accounting have taken the place of hunch, energy and networking.'[365] Thus, even with the successes of 1995, Moss left Ravan at the end of May 1996. He named Monica Seeber as his successor. She was underprepared for the role but attempted to continue in spite of difficult conditions. As she explained, 'Glenn and I have been working together in Ravan for many years, so the focus and ethos of Ravan's publishing is not going to change.'[366] However, within months, plans changed. De Villiers argued, 'To stabilise the situation, we were left with no choice but to embark on a process of rationalisation.'[367] Seeber saw this somewhat differently:

> [O]ur parent company, Hodder & Stoughton Educational, pulled the plug on Ravan because the sales this year had been way below forecast and costs were mounting up alarmingly. We, the Ravan staff, were informed – without any warning – that 'immediate and drastic action' had to be taken, and this amounted to closure of the Ravan offices, dismissal of its entire staff, and absorption of the backlist and perhaps some of the forward publishing into Hodder's own operation.[368]

---

[363] Moss, interview.

[364] David Lea, managing director of Hodder Educational after De Villiers retired, noted that Ravan's average margins had been 40 per cent and 50 per cent while it was part of Hodder, so it had been much more profitable than as an independent publisher, ironically. Minutes of Meeting, 21 June 2000, PMA.

[365] Morphet, 'Child of a special time'.

[366] Seeber to Robert Dudley, 17 May 1996, PMA.

[367] De Villiers, *Mail & Guardian*, November 1996; Gerald de Villiers, interview with author, 11 September 2019.

[368] Seeber to Dan O'Meara, 28 August 1998, PMA.

After a painfully brief opportunity – a few weeks – to seek alternative funding, the staff were dismissed and Ravan passed into the hands of Hodder in August 1996. Seeber speculated, 'Whether it will continue as a publisher, and if it does, as what type of a publisher, is uncertain.'[369] Authors learned of the shift in a letter:

> You have probably heard or read of Ravan's recent financial difficulties, which have made it necessary for the staff to be drastically reduced and for stringent economies to be instituted. But Ravan continues, under its majority shareholder, Hodder and Stoughton, and the Ravan Trust, which constitutes a minority shareholding. . . . The intention is that the Ravan imprint will continue and that new titles consonant with its publishing policy will be brought out. All existing agreements with authors will be honoured. We are hopeful that Ravan Press will continue to make a valuable contribution to South African life over the next quarter-century.[370]

Indeed, in 1997, a collected volume was brought out to commemorate Ravan's twenty-five years. However, there was little new publishing thereafter, and the new titles did not fit the old Ravan list. These included a series on Building Business Skills and one on the Battles of South Africa to capitalise on the 100-year anniversary of the Anglo-Boer War. A few works of fiction, by authors like Mongane Serote and Ahmed Essop, stand out in this patchwork publishing list. Most manuscripts submitted were rejected, with a standard form letter: '(Your manuscript) was reviewed but, given the parlous state of publishing in S.A. at present, it was decided not to proceed with publication.'[371]

The Ravan imprint was further affected by global consolidation, when Macmillan bought Hodder in 2000: 'The year 2000 was an excellent one for Macmillan in terms of both generic growth and acquisition. Hodder & Stoughton, our first acquisition in South Africa, achieved record sales in just

---

[369] Seeber to Dan O'Meara, 28 August 1998, PMA.
[370] De Villiers to authors, 18 April 1997, PMA.   [371] Form letter, 1997, PMA.

seven trading months.'[372] This shows the commitment to profit, in contrast to Ravan's traditions. Reader reports in the archives reflect a changed editorial policy; of one history manuscript, it is said: 'it is the sort of book Ravan would not have hesitated to publish a few years ago, when there was still a strong market for a book of this kind. Unfortunately, it no longer exists.'[373] Authors were very unhappy about the change. Jeff Peires addressed a letter to 'Dear Ravan (or whoever)' and requested that the rights for his works revert to him.[374]

The question was what to do with the imprint and its backlist, especially as it was believed that 'Ravan Press no longer has the cache [sic] it had previously.'[375] Dusanka Stojakovic of Pan Macmillan saw an ideal opportunity to lay the foundations for a new trade imprint. She proposed:

> The ravan imprint and the image of ravan, the publisher of struggle literature has little relevance in south africa today. Many of the titles fall into the 'literary' category and many may be regarded as classics, however despite their stature there is little public interest in works of this kind. Sadly its very important backlist has very little sales potential in the trade market. Many of these books were part of an attempt to bring about political change and have therefore reached their sell-by date.[376]

'(C)an I suggest therefore,' she goes on, 'that we allow the ravan imprint to die a quiet death and that we use the relevant components to build a new entity for the group.' The Ravan list was thus used as a springboard for a new trade list, the Picador Africa imprint, launched in 2004. Both De

---

[372] Denise Diamond to authors, April 2001, PMA.

[373] De Villiers, reader reports, 16 April 2003, PMA.

[374] Jeff Peires to Ravan, 8 January 2001, PMA.

[375] Ed Comm meeting minutes, 21 June 2000, PMA.

[376] 'Picador Africa – proposal for the launch of a new imprint by Pan Macmillan South Africa', 17 October 2002, PMA (punctuation in original).

Villiers and Randall expressed reservations about this decision. But maybe, Randall says now, it had served its purpose.[377]

6 Conclusion

Legacy

The story of Ravan Press does not have a happy ending. It was a small publishing house, produced a few hundred books and proved unsustainable. But Ravan represented something larger. In a context of repression and information control, it played an important role in the cultural and political life of South Africa. Moreover, for a press run by amateurs and activists, it was remarkably successful for a time. This success should be measured not so much in sales as in impact – Ravan, perhaps to a greater extent than any other publisher, created the possibilities for critical writers to emerge and was deliberately provocative in its selection. Its aim was to publish critical voices, progressive ideas and books that gave ordinary people a sense of their power and, through this means, to contribute to the struggle against apartheid – speaking truth to power, as Edward Said puts it. Running the Press involved a delicate balancing act between commercial viability and radical publishing, but the emphasis always fell on the writers. For those involved, publishing was neither a profession nor a calling, but a means to an end – achieving the overturn of apartheid. The highly committed staff thus helped develop an oppositional print culture: they created networks, experimented with format and genre, produced important books and punched above their weight in terms of visibility. Unlike samizdat or underground publishing, though, Ravan operated openly. It was frequently targeted by the government, out of all proportion to its actual size or output.

The lasting impact of an oppositional publisher is difficult to measure, but Ravan helped shape attitudes to change. Peter Randall, for instance, argues that 'Ravan publications did much to rephrase the debate about the South African past and to bring into focus earlier struggles against oppression.'[378] The publications were widely read among anti-apartheid

---

[377] Randall, interview.   [378] Randall, 'The Beginnings of Ravan Press', 31.

activists and aspiring writers; Tony Morphet suggests that Ravan was 'a remarkable invention that changed the meaning of books for a generation of South Africans'.[379] As a result, it 'played an important role in building the awareness, ideas and committed action that put an end to apartheid'.[380] Apart from its political role, Ravan is remembered primarily for its literary publishing; indeed, in a survey conducted by the *Mail & Guardian* newspaper in 1997, half of the best South African authors voted for had been published at some time by Ravan. While Ravan is perhaps best known for *Staffrider* and its literary titles, fiction made up only around a third of the list (rising to nearly half under Kirkwood's stewardship). The non-fiction titles, often aimed at a non-academic audience or telling the stories of ordinary people, had just as significant an impact.

One of the ways in which the lasting impact of a publisher can be traced is through the number of books still in print. In around twenty-five years, Ravan published more than 300 titles. Some of these are particularly notable, for instance, the publishing of two Nobel Prize winners, Nadine Gordimer and J.M. Coetzee. The latter's career may have taken much longer to get off the ground without the support for his debut novel, *Dusklands*. Ravan also recognised the potential of Miriam Tlali, one of the earliest black women to be published in South Africa. Other examples include Wopko Jensma's innovative blend of writing and artwork, while Essop Patel's work on Nat Nakasa and Brian Willan's on Sol Plaatje kept these writers alive for a new generation. Chabani Manganyi's work is still in print, with a new edition of his 1978 title *Being-Black-in-the-World* published in 2019. Peter Randall's legacy lies in the lasting influence of such writers, as well as his ability to see the need for a critical publisher and to take that opportunity — at some personal cost.

His successor, Mike Kirkwood, developed a remarkable network and a vision of writing for liberation. While the collective structure he initiated cannot be called successful, the energy and dynamism that suffused the informal office set up served as a catalyst for the publishing of innovative and daring work. The magazine Kirkwood and Mothobi Mutloatse founded, *Staffrider*, gave its name to a generation of young, black writers

---

[379] Morphet, 'Child of a Special Time'. [380] Cloete, 'Alternative Publishing', 43.

and also served as an incubator for book-length writing. Building on an existing tradition of literary magazines, *Staffrider* amplified their reach and standing. Titles by Ahmed Essop, Njabulo Ndebele, Achmat Dangor, Ellen Kuzwayo and others remain in print, some on the Picador Africa list. While the Ravan editorial team commissioned few titles, their selection remained remarkably consistent with their expressed mission. This mission was deliberately non-racial and unaligned with any specific political party. In practice, this meant that space was given to both black and white authors, even though black authors were specially courted. They were less successful in terms of staff composition, with the directors remaining white (and men, until Monica Seeber's short term in the 1990s). The readership, too, despite intense efforts to reach a broader market, was inevitably limited by social divisions, access to booksellers and language. In other words, the idealism that supported this freewheeling venture could not escape the pressures of the stratified apartheid society. This is perhaps most clearly embodied in the split with Skotaville. The balancing act between white ownership and black expression could only be sustained up to a point.

In the late 1980s, after Kirkwood's exit and the collapse of the collective structure, Ravan lost its way to a large extent. As commercial imperatives became more important and funding dwindled, Glenn Moss and his team attempted to refocus Ravan by publishing socially relevant titles for the 'new South Africa'. It is clear that as the publisher became more professional and more focused on viability, it lost the essence of what had made it unique. Ravan had expected to have political credibility in the new South Africa and thus access to more lucrative markets, but its ability to adapt to more commercial realities was limited. At the same time, the space in which Ravan operated was increasingly co-opted by more mainstream publishers; this attempt to commodify alternative audiences saw a number of authors who had been oppositional later being published as part of mainstream lists. By being taken over by corporate interests that did not share their ideals, the legacy of oppositional publishing was not carried through into the new South Africa.

From Political to Commercial

What do oppositional publishers do when their battle is won? Ravan's mission had been protest and engagement; after 1994, organisations that had previously opposed the apartheid government had to shift focus rapidly to a discourse of transformation and reconciliation. Many mainstream publishers managed to adapt, through partnerships, black empowerment deals and vigorous lobbying. But no oppositional publishers survived unscathed into the twenty-first century. As the marketplace became more commercially oriented and hostile to cultural and political idealism, they became unsustainable. Ravan sold a majority shareholding to Hodder & Stoughton Educational in 1994, having survived just long enough to see the new South Africa come into being. After being bought out by Macmillan, it was allowed to fade away, with its backlist serving as a starting point for a new imprint. Taurus ceased publishing in the early 1990s, and Human & Rousseau bought its stock. David Philip survives as an imprint of New Africa Books, after the Philips retired in late 1999. Skotaville lives on in a different form, as part of a media firm, the Mutloatse Art Heritage Trust. None of these is still an active, productive publisher. The new generation of 'born-frees' (those born after 1994) thus has no experience of this kind of independent, progressive publishing. What does this tell us about the role of publishing for social change in today's world?

In most contexts, the main ideological poles are commerce and culture. In the South African case – as in other countries with histories of state suppression – politics must be added to this mix. In fact, it is often the overriding factor underlying decisions about what and who to publish. Pierre Bourdieu makes a distinction between those publishers that are willing to take a risk with new authors, for long-term gain, and those that prefer to publish established, best-seller authors, for mass consumption and short-term gain.[381] Oppositional publishers fall on the side of long-term gain, but in their case the focus is political change and social relevance, rather than either literary merit or commercial profits. However, the biggest shift in the publishing industry over the past decades has been the embrace of commercialism. André Schiffrin refers to this as the replacement of state censorship by 'market censorship', as the commercial ideology infiltrates all aspects of book publishing.[382] As a result, the obstacles faced by those

---

[381] Bourdieu, 'Market of Symbolic Goods'. [382] Schiffrin, *Business of Books*.

wanting to promote progressive and radical views have also changed. Publishers that advocate a political mission rather than profit have become anachronisms, a quaint and unprofessional oddity. However, seeing publishers as primarily commercial should not imply that they do not still promote certain political and cultural ideologies through the works they publish – they do. Even as commercial publishers make seemingly aesthetic and financial decisions about what to publish, they are also making cultural judgements that imply a moral and ideological position.[383] The publishing world remains largely white, privileged and cautious about social criticism. Therefore, there is still a need for committed, alternative publishers to make available groundbreaking and controversial authors not being published by the mainstream publishers.

In South Africa, few publishers have emerged to take up the mantle of Ravan and the other oppositional publishers. The current commercial publishing context has been described as having 'regressed, in terms of diversity in ownership, as well as in the variety of its output'.[384] In addition, the new government had (and still has) no interest in local publishing. Andries Oliphant drew up a call to action for publishers in the early 1990s, and it is startling to observe how many of the points he raised remain relevant and necessary: he spoke, for instance, of the need for South African publishers to advocate and defend the right of the reading public to have access to all published material and information and to give space to subordinate classes, such as workers and gender groups, to articulate their interests and conceptions of what freedom and social justice might mean to them.[385] The ideal of free access to a range of ideas to inform a democratic society, which lies at the heart of oppositional print culture, has become elusive once more.

[383] McLaughlin, 'Oppositional aesthetics', 175.
[384] Oliphant, 'From Colonialism to Democracy', 121.
[385] Oliphant, 'South African publishers'.

Bibliography

Acknowledgements: This work is based on research supported in part by the National Research Foundation of South Africa (Grant Number 103730) and the British Academy's Newton Mobility Grant. Thanks to all the archivists and those who agreed to be interviewed for this research.

Archives

Ravan Press collection, 1998.8. NELM (Amazwi) Archives, Grahamstown/ Makhanda, South Africa.

Ravan Press collection, Pan Macmillan Archives, Johannesburg, South Africa. (Uncatalogued)

Secondary Sources

Africa Legal Assistance Project. (1974). *Interim Report*. Washington, DC: ALAP.

Albert, Michael. (2008). Interview: Alternative publishing and its problems. *ZNet*, 18 February.

Alvarez-Pereyre, Jacques. (1984). *The Poetry of Commitment in South Africa*. Johannesburg: Heinemann.

American Library Association. (1980). *Alternatives in Print*. New York: Neal-Schuman.

Banoobhai, Shabbir. Online: http://veilsoflight.com/about/.

Barnett, Ursula. (1983). *A Vision of Order*. Amherst: University of Massachusetts Press.

Benjamin, Walter. (1973). The storyteller. In Gregory Polletta, ed., *Issues in Contemporary Literary Criticism*. Boston: Little, Brown & Co.

Booth-Yudelman, Gillian. (1997). South African political prison-literature between 1948 and 1990. Diss., Unisa.

Bourdieu, Pierre. (1985). The Market of Symbolic Goods. *Poetics* 14(1/2): 13–44.

Bozzoli, Belinda. (1983). *Town and Countryside in the Transvaal*. History Workshop *2* (Wits University).

— (1990). Intellectuals, Audiences and Histories. *Radical History Review*, 46–47: 237–63.

Breckenridge, Keith. (2015). Hopeless Entanglement: The Short History of the Academic Humanities in South Africa. *American Historical Review*, 120(4): 1253–66.

Brummer, William. (1990). Violence Processing: Fighting Words and South Africa. *Processed World*, 25 (Fall).

Bryer, Lynne. (1982). Publishing in the wake of Soweto. *The Bookseller*, 15 July: 129.

Callinicos, Luli. (1990). Popular History in the Eighties. *Radical History Review*, 46(7): 285–97.

Chapman, Michael. (1981). South Africa: The Year That Was. *Kunapipi*, 3(1).

— (1982). South Africa: The Year That Was. *Kunapipi*, 4(1).

Chisholm, Linda. (2013). The Textbook Saga and Corruption in Education. *Southern African Review of Education* 19(1): 7–22.

Cloete, Dick. (2000). Alternative Publishing in South Africa in the 1970s and 1980s. In Nicholas Evans & Monica Seeber (eds), *The Politics of Publishing in South Africa*. Pietermaritzburg: University of Natal Press.

Connor, Bernard. (1986). Remembering the Freedom Charter. *Grace & Truth*, 3: 112.

Davis, Geoffrey. (2003). *Voices of Justice and Reason*. Amsterdam: Rodopi.

De Lange, Margreet. (1997). *The Muzzled Muse*. Amsterdam: John Benjamins.

De Waal, Shaun. (1996). Ravan will NOT close. *Mail & Guardian*, 8 November.

Douyère, David & Pinhas, Luc. (2008). L'accès à la parole: la publication politique des éditeurs indépendants. *Communication & langages*, 156 (June): 75–89.

Downing, John. (1984). *The Political Experience of Alternative Communication*. Boston: South End Press.

— (2001). *Radical Media: Rebellious Communication and Social Movements*. Thousand Oaks, CA: Sage.

Driver, Dorothy. (1987). Appendix II: South Africa. *Journal of Commonwealth Literature*: 170–98. https://doi.org/10.1177/002198948802300211

— (1989/90). Appendix II: South Africa. *Journal of Commonwealth Literature*: 168–213. https://doi.org/10.1177/002198948802300211

Dubow, Saul. (2014). *Apartheid 1948–1994*. New York: Oxford University Press.

Efrat, Z. (1996). New ownership scramble. *Natal Witness*, 27 November: 8.

Egan, Anthony. (1990). Perspectives of the future. *The Cape Argus*, 26 February.

Enzensberger, Hans. (1976). *Raids and Reconstructions: Essays on Politics, Crime and Culture*. London: Pluto Press.

Essery, Isabel. (2005). The impact of politics on indigenous independent publishers from 1970–2004. Diss., Oxford Brookes University.

Frederikse, Julie. (2015). Author's reflections: Southern African mashups. Online: www.saha.org.za/nonracialism/authors_reflections_september_2015.htm

Gqola, Pumla Dineo. (2001). In Search of Female Staffriders: Authority, Gender and Audience, 1978–1982, *Current Writing* 13 (2): 31–41.

Gray, Stephen. (1980). Southern Africa: The Year That Was. *Kunapipi*, 2(1).

Greyling, L.-M. (2003). Redefining the dialogue of criticism. MA Diss., University of Pretoria.

Gwala, Mafika. (1984). Writing as a Cultural Weapon. In M. J. Daymond, J.U. Jacobs & Margaret Lenta (eds). *Momentum: On Recent South African Writing*. Pietermaritzburg: University of Natal Press, 37–53.

Hacksley, Malcolm. (2007). An Oppositional Publisher under a Repressive Regime. Paper presented at A World Elsewhere conference, Cape Town.

Hadfield, Leslie Anne. (2016). *Liberation and Development*. East Lansing: Michigan State University Press.

Hall, Stuart. (1973/1980). Encoding/Decoding. In Stuart Hall, Dorothy Hobson, Andrew Lowe & Paul Willis (eds). *Culture, Media, Language*. London: Hutchinson.

Hayes, Graham. (2016). Chabani Manganyi: Black intellectual and psychologist. *Psychology in Society*, 52, 73-9.

Hill, Shannen. (2015). *The Iconography of Black Consciousness: Biko's Ghost*. Minneapolis: University of Minnesota Press.

Hofmeyr, Isabel. (1992). Review. *Weekly Mail*, October 30 to November 5.

Horn, Peter. (1994). *Writing My Reading: Essays on Literary Politics in South Africa*. Amsterdam: Rodopi.

Hotz, Paul. (1991). Publishers' problems bad news for writers. *The Daily News*, 26 September: 22.

International Commission of Jurists. (1975). *The Trial of Beyers Naudé*. London: Search Press.

Ireland, Philippa. (2013). Laying the Foundations: New Beacon Books, Bogle L'Ouverture Press and the Politics of Black British Publishing. *E-rea* 11(1).

Isaacson, Maureen. (1996). A quirky, subversive voice in local literature. *Saturday Star*, 1 June.

Kannemeyer, J.C. (2012). *J.M. Coetzee, A Life in Writing*. London: Scribe.

Kantey, Mike. (1990). Foreword: Publishing in South Africa. In *Africa Bibliography 1989*. London: International African Institute.

— (1992). The provision of textbooks in South Africa. National Education Policy Investigation working paper.

Keaney, Matthew. (2010). From the Sophiatown Shebeens to the Streets of Soweto on the pages of *Drum, The Classic, New Classic*, and *Staffrider*. Diss., George Mason University.

Kellner, Clive & Gonzalez, Sergio-Albio, eds. (2009). *Thami Mnyele + Medu*. Johannesburg: Jacana.

Khan, Shafa. (1989). Who reads what's written to be watched? *Weekly Mail*, 23–30 March.

Khoapa, Bennie. (1973). *Black Review*. Durban: Spro-cas Black Community Programme.

Kirkwood, Mike. (1976). The Colonizer: A Critique of the English South African Cultural Theory. In *Poetry South Africa*. Johannesburg: Ad Donker.

— (1979). Banning of Book Angers Africans. *The Argus*, 14 November.

— (1980). *Staffrider*: An informal discussion. *English in Africa* 7(2).

— (1983). Reflections on PEN. *Sesame*, 3 (Summer): 22–6.

— (1987). Literature and Popular Culture in South Africa. *Third World Quarterly* 9(2).

Kleinschmidt, Horst. (2013). Roots and journeys linking the Christian Institute and wider community to the re-ignition of resistance to apartheid in the early 70's. Unpublished document.

Kleyn, Leti & Marais, Johann Lodewyk. (2009). Wopko Jensma en die sensuurwetgewing van die jare sewentig. *Tydskrif vir Nederlands en Afrikaans* 16(20): 37–52.

Kunene, Daniel. (1981). Ideas under Arrest: Censorship in South Africa. *Research in African Literatures* 12(4).

Le Roux, Elizabeth. (2018). Miriam Tlali and Ravan Press: Politics and Power in Literary Publishing during the Apartheid Period. *Journal of Southern African Studies*, 44(3): 431–44.

Lewis, Simon. (2000). Review of *Ravan Twenty-Five Years*, H-Net.

MacKenzie, Craig. (1990). Njabulo Ndebele and the Challenge of the New. *Language Projects Review* 5(3).

Matshoba, Mtutuzeli. (1981). Disbandment of PEN. *Staffrider* 4(1).

Matteau, Rachel. (2007). The readership for banned literature and its underground networks in apartheid South Africa. *Innovation* 35(1).

Maués, Flamarion. (2014). Livros, editoras e oposição à ditadura. *Estudos avançados* 28(80): 91–104.

McClintock, Anne. (1987). *Azikwelwa*: Politics and Value in Black South African Poetry. *Critical Inquiry* 13 (Spring): 597–623.

McDonald, Peter. (2009). *The Literature Police*. Oxford: Oxford University Press.

McGuinness, Patrick. (2015). *Poetry and Radical Politics in Fin de Siècle France*. Oxford: Oxford University Press.

McLaughlin, Robert. (1996). Oppositional Aesthetics/Oppositional Ideologies: A Brief Cultural History of Alternative Publishing in the United States. *Critique: Studies in Contemporary Fiction* 37(3).

McMillian, John. (2011). *Smoking Typewriters: The Sixties Underground Press and the Rise of Alternative Media in America*. New York: Oxford University Press.

Medeiros, Nuno. (2015). Action, Reaction and Protest by Publishers in 1960s Portugal. *Politics, Religion & Ideology*, 16(2–3).

Mitchell, James. (1992). Top of the list in the publishing stakes. *The Star*, 12 August.

Mofokeng, Boitumelo. (1989). Where Are the Women? Ten Years of *Staffrider*. *Current Writing* 1(1): 41–3.

Morphet, Tony. (1978). Introduction. In R. Turner, ed., *The Eye of the Needle*. Johannesburg: Ravan.

— (1996). Ravan: Child of a special time. *Mail & Guardian*, 1–7 November.

Moss, Glenn. (1993a). Educational Publishing in South Africa. *African Publishing Review*.

— (1993b). The Life and Changing Times of an Independent Publisher in South Africa. *Logos* 4(3).

— (1994). The Life and Times of Ravan. *African Publishing Review* (May/June).

— (1997). Ringing the Changes: Twenty-Five Years of Ravan Press. In Gerald de Villiers, ed., *Ravan Twenty-five Years*. Johannesburg: Ravan Press.

Mpe, Phaswane & Seeber, Monica. (2000). The Politics of Book Publishing in South Africa. In Nicholas Evans & Monica Seeber, eds., *The Politics of Publishing in South Africa*. Pietermaritzburg: University of Natal Press.

Mtshali, Oswald. (1980). Ravan: Pressing for change . . . *Tribune*, 19 August.

Mzamane, Mbulelo, ed. (1986). *Hungry Flames and Other Black South African Short Stories*. Harlow: Longman.

— (1991). The Impact of Black Consciousness on Culture. In N.B. Pityana, M. Ramphele, M. Mpumlwana & L. Wilson, eds., *Bounds of Possibility: The Legacy of Steve Biko and Black Consciousness*. London: Zed.

Ndebele, Njabulo. (1983). Life-Sustaining Poetry of a Fghting People. *Staffrider* 5(3): 44–5.

— (1989). The Writers' Movement in South Africa. *Research in African Literatures*, 20(3): 412–21.

Nicol, Mike. (1975). Ravan flies out of the red. *To the Point*, 8 August.

— (2009). A chat with Wessel Ebersohn. CrimeBeat. http://crimebeat .bookslive.co.za/blog/2009/08/25/a-chat-with-wessel-ebersohn/

Nkosi, Lewis. (1994). Constructing the 'Cross-Border' Reader. In E. Boehmer, L. Chrisman & K. Parker, eds., *Altered State? Writing and South Africa*. Aarhus: Dangaroo Press, 45–46.

O'Toole, Sean. (2017). Uncommon Criticism: Reading Ivan Vladislavić's Collected Work as Art Criticism. *Journal of Commonwealth Literature*, 52(1): 11–26.

Oliphant, Andries. (1990). *Staffrider* Magazine and Popular History. *Radical History Review* 46/47.

— (1991). South African Publishers, Social Transformation and the Democratisation of Communication. *Communicatio* 17(1).

— (1998). *Celebrating Nadine Gordimer*. New York: Viking.

— (2000). From Colonialism to Democracy: Writers and Publishing in South Africa. In Gerald de Villiers, ed. *The Politics of Publishing in South Africa*. Pietermaritzburg: University of Natal Press.

— (2001). Forums and Forces. In Kirsten Holst Petersen & Anna Rutherford, eds. *On Shifting Sands*. Portsmouth, NH: Heinemann.

Omond, Roger. (1985). Battle of the books. *The Guardian*, 17 May.

Penfold, Thomas. (2013). Black Consciousness and the Politics of Writing the Nation in South Africa. Diss., University of Birmingham.

Philip, David. (1991). Book Publishing Under and After Apartheid. In *Book Publishing in South Africa for the 1990s*. Cape Town: National Library of South Africa.

Povey, John. (1985). Review. *African Book Publishing Record*, 11(2).

Powell, Rose. (1980). Writing Is Part of the Struggle. *Index on Censorship* 9(6): 10.

Prabhakaran, S. (1998). Crisis hits educational publishers. *Mail & Guardian*, 17–23 April.

Pretorius, William. (1994). Local publishers in flux. *Mail & Guardian*, 27 May–2 June: 38.

Randall, Peter. (1970). *Anatomy of Apartheid*. Johannesburg: Spro-cas.

— (1973a). *A Taste of Power*. Johannesburg: Spro-cas.

— (1973b). Spro-Cas: Motivations and Assumptions. *Pro Veritate*, 5.

— (1974). Spro-Cas: Some Publishing Problems. *Africa Today* 21(2): 75–78.

— (1975). Minority Publishing in South Africa. *African Book Publishing Record* 1(3): 219–22.

— (1976). The Banning of Confused Mhlaba. *Index on Censorship* 5(4): 6–9.

— (1997). The Beginnings of Ravan Press: A Memoir. In G.E. de Villiers, ed. *Ravan Twenty-Five Years*. Johannesburg: Ravan Press.

Rantete, Johannes. (1985). 'The Third Day of September'. *Index on Censorship* 14(3): 37–42.

Rich, Paul. (1993). *Hope and Despair: English-Speaking Intellectuals and South African Politics, 1896–1976*. London: British Academic Press.

Rive, Richard. (1979/2002). Interview. In Bernth Lindfors, ed. *Africa Talks Back*. Trenton, NJ: African World Press.

Roberts, Ronald Suresh. (2005). *No Cold Kitchen*. Johannesburg: STE Publishers.

Schiffrin, André. (2001). *The Business of Books*. London: Verso.

Schreiber, Rachael, ed. (2013). *Modern Print Activism in the United States*. Abingdon: Ashgate.

Schwartz, Pat. (1981). Ravan: Letting the cats out of the bag. *Rand Daily Mail*, 13 November: 11.

— (1984). Books putting black views into words. *The Star*.

Schweitzer, Janina. (2008). The Marketing Strategies and the Generation of Publishing Plans in Spanish Publishing Houses with a View to the Censorship and Economic Policy Employed during Francoism (1939–1975). *Alles Buch*, XXVII.

Seeber, Monica. (1996). An Appeal by Ravan Press. *African Book Publishing Record* 22(3).

Segal, Aaron. (1985). Review. *African Book Publishing Record* 11.

Sepamla, Sipho. (1976). The Black Writer in South Africa Today: Problems and Dilemmas. *New Classic* 3.

— (1980). A Note on New Classic and S'Ketsh. *English in Africa*, 7(2).

Seroke, Jaki. (1984). The Voice of the Voiceless. *African Book Publishing Record* 10(4): 201–6.

Sheik, Ayub. (2002). 'I feel like hollerin but the town is too small': A Biographical Study of Wopko Jensma. *Alternation*, 9(2): 236–76.

Smaldone, Joseph. (1991). Review. *African Book Publishing Record*.

Sole, Kelwyn. (2001). Political Fiction, Representation and the Canon. *English in Africa* 28(2).

Stadler, Alf. (1975). Anxious Radicals: SPRO-CAS and the Apartheid Society. *Journal of Southern African Studies* 2(1).

Suttie, M.-L. (2005). The Formative Years of the University of South Africa Library, 1946 to 1976. *Mousaion*, 23(1).

Trimbur, John. (2009). Popular Literacy and the Resources of Print Culture. *College Composition and Communication*, 61(1): 85–108.

Van Slambrouck, Paul. (1984). Black South African Writers 'Break Free,' Publish Own Books. *Christian Science Monitor*, 16 April.

Van Wyk, Chris. (1988). *Staffrider* and the Politics of Culture. In Gerald de Villiers, ed. *Ravan Twenty-Five Years*. Johannesburg: Ravan.

Vaughan, Michael. (1984). *Staffrider* and Directions within Contemporary South African Literature. In Landeg White & Tim Couzens, eds. *Literature and Society in South Africa*. Cape Town: Maskew Miller Longman.

Vladislavic, Ivan. (2008). Staffrider. *Chimurenga* (March). Online: https://chimurengachronic.co.za/staffrider.

Vladislavic, Ivan. (2014). A vivid voice. *Sunday Times*, 12 October.

Vladislavic, Ivan & Oliphant, Andries. (1988). Prologue. In *Ten Years of Staffrider, 1978–1988*. Johannesburg: Ravan.

Watts, Jane. (1989). *Black Writers from South Africa: Towards a Discourse of Liberation*. Basingstoke: Macmillan.

Wessels, E.M. (1988). The challenge and the crisis facing the educational publishing industry in the dissemination of information in South Africa. MA Diss, University of Pretoria.

Wittenberg, Hermann. (2008). The Taint of the Censor. *English in Africa*, 35(2): 133–50.

Young, John K. (2006). *Black Writers, White Publishers*. Oxford: University of Mississippi Press.

Zwi, Rose. (2006). In conversation with Mothobi Mutloatse. *LitNet*. Online: https://argief.litnet.co.za/article.php?news_id=2943.

Cambridge Elements ≡

Publishing and Book Culture

SERIES EDITOR
Samantha Rayner
University College London

Samantha Rayner is a Reader in UCL's Department of Information Studies. She is also Director of UCL's Centre for Publishing, co-Director of the Bloomsbury CHAPTER (Communication History, Authorship, Publishing, Textual Editing and Reading) and co-editor of the Academic Book of the Future BOOC (Book as Open Online Content) with UCL Press.

ASSOCIATE EDITOR
Leah Tether
University of Bristol

Leah Tether is Professor of Medieval Literature and Publishing at the University of Bristol. With an academic background in medieval French and English literature and a professional background in trade publishing, Leah has combined her expertise and developed an international research profile in book and publishing history from manuscript to digital.

ABOUT THE SERIES

This series aims to fill the demand for easily accessible, quality texts available for teaching and research in the diverse and dynamic fields of Publishing and Book Culture. Rigorously researched and peer-reviewed Elements will be published under themes, or 'Gatherings'. These Elements should be the first check point for researchers or students working on that area of publishing and book trade history and practice: we hope that, situated so logically at Cambridge University Press, where academic publishing in the UK began, it will develop to create an unrivalled space where these histories and practices can be investigated and preserved.

Cambridge Elements ≡

Publishing and Book Culture

COLONIAL AND POST-COLONIAL PUBLISHING
Gathering Editor: Caroline Davis
Caroline Davis is Senior Lecturer in the Oxford International Centre for Publishing at Oxford Brookes University. She is the author of *Creating Postcolonial Literature: African Writers and British Publishers* (Palgrave, 2013), the editor of *Print Cultures: A Reader in Theory and Practice* (Macmillan, 2019) and co-editor of *The Book in Africa: Critical Debates* (Palgrave, 2015).

ELEMENTS IN THE GATHERING

A full series listing is available at: www.cambrige.org/EPBC

Printed in the United States
By Bookmasters